Easeful
death

Caring for dying & bereaved people

703

Easeful death

Caring for dying & bereaved people

Jeanne Katz and Moyra Sidell

Hodder & Stoughton

A MEMBER OF THE HODDER HEADLINE GROUP

British Library Cataloguing in Publication Data
Katz, J.
  Easeful Death: Caring for Dying and
  Bereaved People
  I. Title II. Sidell, M.
  362.175

ISBN 0 340 59514 0

First published 1994
Impression number   10 9 8 7 6 5 4 3 2 1
Year   1999 1998 1997 1996 1995 1994

Typeset by Wearset, Boldon, Tyne and Wear.
Printed in Great Britain for Hodder & Stoughton Educational, a division of Hodder Headline
Plc, 338 Euston Road, London NW1 3BH by Page Bros (Norwich) Ltd.

Darkling I listen; and, for many a time
I have been half in love with easeful Death,
Call'd him soft names in many a mused rhyme,
To take into the air my quiet breath;
Now more than ever seems it rich to die,
To cease upon the midnight with no pain,
While thou art pouring thy soul abroad
In such an ecstasy!

JOHN KEATS, 'ODE TO A NIGHTINGALE'

Contents

Acknowledgements

Our colleagues at the Open University who constituted the 'Death and Dying' course team, Margaret Allott, Donna Dickenson, Malcolm Johnson and Alyson Peberdy, all contributed in different ways to the development of our thinking. In relation to the preparation of this book we should like to thank Alyson Peberdy who made helpful comments on an earlier draft of this book. Bridget Lovell, who has worked as an oncology sister, palliative care nurse, health visitor and practice nurse also read an earlier draft and from a nursing perspective made useful suggestions. Our thanks also to Christine Jones for preparing the drafts.

1

Facing death and dying

We took the title of our book from the verse of the poem that forms our epigraph, written by John Keats who was at the time suffering from consumption. We liked the image of an 'easeful' death and felt that looking at ways of 'easing' death for those dying and those bereaved was what we were aiming to do in this book. Helping someone to experience an 'easeful' death is certainly not an 'easy' task and there are situations which can make this impossible. Moreover, we may find it hard to agree on what constitutes an 'easeful' death. But that in itself is part of the task: to help people as far as possible to die the way they would choose, whether it be in sorrow, anger or tranquillity, oblivion or acute awareness, alone or surrounded by loved ones. Similarly, easing the path of bereavement will involve helping people to find their own ways of relating to their grief.

This book is addressed specifically to those whose jobs bring them into contact with dying and bereaved people. But the context within which they work, the attitudes and beliefs which they bring to their work as well as the attitudes and beliefs of those who are dying or bereaved will all affect the way in which they can help make death and grief as 'easeful' as possible.

A death–denying society?

It is often said that our society is 'death-denying': that people avoid thinking about death, they don't talk about death, that death is a 'taboo' subject and that this has harmful consequences for those who are dying or grieving.

The notion that we are a death-denying society has been debated since the 1960s when two influential writers, Philippe Aries and Geoffrey Gorer, claimed that in contrast to earlier historical periods death had become an unmentionable topic. Geoffrey Gorer pointed out that we seem to have a fascination with violent deaths. He based this observation on the numbers of shootings, killings and brutal deaths depicted in our mass media in detective stories, Westerns, spy stories, war stories, horror stories and science fiction. Yet, he claimed, natural death is hardly ever portrayed. An American study done in 1971 found that by the time a child in the US reaches the age of 14 they are likely to have witnessed on average 18,000 people killed on television. In contrast the average American will reach the age of 40 before encountering a real death of someone close to them.

One of the reasons why we may be finding it hard to face death is because it has become a remote event. No longer 'in the midst of life are we in death'. We have a reasonable expectation that we will live out our 'span' and a little bit more. We certainly do not expect our children to die before us and most women do not see death as a possible outcome of pregnancy. The past century has witnessed decreases in the rates of morbidity and mortality. Contagious diseases which used to ravage societies have been virtually eradicated. Even in locations where infectious diseases have persisted, the availability of curative medications such as antibiotics has significantly increased the chances of survival. Until the AIDS epidemic began, involving a younger age group, death occurred predominantly in old age, when people die primarily from chronic, degenerative conditions of the cardiovascular system and secondarily from malignancies. Hence death is no longer the outcome of rapid-onset, acute diseases but rather a lengthy process most common among older people. Life expectancy has risen dramatically over the past century with the expected life span in Britain having increased from 51.5 years for males and 55.4 years for females in 1910–12 (quoted in Seale 1993) to 72.3 years for males and 78.2 years for females in 1991 (Central Statistical Office 1992). This increase in life expectancy, coupled with the decrease in the number of people living in each dwelling, means that most older people in Britain today tend to live either alone or only with their spouse. As in other western industrialised nations, the population in the UK includes a substantial proportion of older people, many of whom are retired and who suffer from chronic medical conditions.

In addition to advances in medical technology, such as the development of vaccines and antibiotics, several cultural, social and economic factors have contributed to these changes in the rates of morbidity and mortality and are possibly as important. These include progress in the fields of nutrition, sanitation and housing. The number of people occupying each dwelling has fallen; this means that, on the one hand, less overcrowding may facilitate better living conditions, increased privacy and preservation of dignity; on the other, with more people living alone, there are fewer carers available.

Another reason why we may avoid death is because even when it does occur it is hidden away and separated from life. Philippe Ariès argued that we conceal death by:

- talking about illness with an expectation of cure but disgust at the 'dirtiness' of death;
- locating dying people in hospitals away from public view;
- the regulation and organisation of death by doctors for whom death is a failure.

Since the mid-nineteenth century health care in western societies has been transformed. Hitherto, rites of passage from birth to death took place in people's homes surrounded by their families, neighbours and occasionally local midwives. Dying was commonplace at all ages: for example, maternal and infant mortality were known risks of pregnancy. Families were larger and many generations occupied the same dwelling. As the domestic environment was the site of most health care, death was a routine and public occurrence observed by all, including children. In theory, the different generations with whom they shared their lodgings provided the practical care for dying relatives, but whether good care was available depended on social and financial circumstances.

Today, instead of death being everybody's business, it has become the special concern of the medical profession.

The professionalisation of death and dying

Death and dying have not always been seen as requiring the intervention of medical, paramedical and other professional staff. In contemporary Britain we tend to accept the notion that deaths are classified according to a physical cause, thus in a 'medical' framework, but this has not always been so. Till the late middle ages in the western world, death was regarded primarily as an act of God and beyond the interference of man; death was seen as a punishment for social or moral misdemeanours. Untimely death was sometimes attributed to the intervention of witch doctors or spirits, if not as a sentence from God, and certainly could not be prevented by human actions. Nowadays westerners view death as a medical event with a physical cause rather than the result of factors beyond the control of ordinary people. Death is seen as a disease rather than the normal expiry of life. The past hundred years have witnessed a change in the way in which control over health in general, not just death and dying, has become professionalised, with power vested in the medical and paramedical occupations, rather than in the family. This 'medicalisation' has changed the ways in which health care is delivered. As the profession of medicine grew stronger it began to focus on alleviating symptoms and strive to find cures for diseases, particularly those likely to result in death. Research endeavours became central to medical practice, with efforts directed at understanding disease processes in order to combat them rather than at providing comfort and care. These efforts required a laboratory base, and so much health care became centralised in the hospital sector. Although primary health care continued to be delivered in the community by general practitioners and other health workers, seriously ill people were believed to be best cared for in hospital, and the site of death was thus removed from the household. Links can be made between the denial of death and where death takes place. As professionals increasingly became involved in caring for dying people, terminally ill people were transferred into hospitals and thus removed from everyday life. As noted earlier, this movement to the hospital sector must be seen in the context of wider social changes such as increased longevity, smaller family units and increased incidence of older people living alone.

Current legislation requires death to be certified according to physical cause, diagnosed by a medical practitioner. David Armstrong (1987), a sociologist writing on the subject, believes that it is since the introduction of the legal requirement that deaths should be registered and recorded centrally that death has become a more medical and legal matter. The concern to determine the cause of death focuses more on dead or dying bodies than dying people. Along with this medicalisation of death has come the professionalisation of disposal of the body. Once a person is pronounced dead, the corpse is no longer the responsibility of the family: it is handed over to another relatively new occupation – the undertaker, or funeral director. In Britain until the end of the nineteenth century either female relatives of the deceased or midwives laid out the bodies of the dead. Individual tradesmen were used to provide the goods needed for the funeral, which was usually conducted by a local clergyman. The profession of undertaking developed at the same time as a weakening of social networks, which hitherto had created a structure within which local communities functioned. Where strong social networks flourish, even today in some cultures, local people still organise the trappings for funerals, which may be quite elaborate, without the help of undertakers or their equivalent. The actual ceremonies often take place within the auspices and with the support of the local Christian church, while incorporating some local customs. As the occupation of undertaking developed, so the belief took hold that only specially trained professionals were competent to deal with corpses. Hence control over the body moved from families and communities to a service group who had particular skills to market, as well as professional interests to satisfy.

As well as the unfamiliarity of death and its concealment, there is thought to be another factor which indicates that we are a death-denying society. That is the lack of rituals in modern western societies. Mourning rituals serve to affirm religious and cultural group identity which might be threatened by death, but these have become largely redundant as society has taken on an increasingly individualistic and secular character. The formality of rituals is alien to many in modern society, where informality is preferred in order to break down the barriers between people. But ironically, in the case of death and dying it is often the lack of an accepted formula for talking about death which leaves people feeling that they 'don't know what to say'.

To speak of death

We spend a large proportion of our national wealth on preventing death; although we know that it is inevitable, we do our best to delay it for as long as possible and so we postpone all thoughts of death. In fact, we seem to have a curious feeling that if we do not talk about it, it will not come our way. Talking about death, actually using the words 'death' and 'dying' is felt by many people to bring death nearer, whether it is our own or that of someone close to us, as though the words themselves have some power over life and death. The way we use the language of death and dying indicates that we are happy to use the words in other contexts, such as 'I'm dying to see you' or 'I'm dead tired' or 'I'm pleased to death', but that we often resort to euphemism when we are actually referring to death, dying or the dead. The following list of euphemisms for the words 'death' and 'dying', some humorous, some simply avoidance metaphors, indicates how hard people find it to use the actual words.

Humorous	*Avoidance metaphors*
snuff it	passed away/on/over
shuffle off	deceased
kick the bucket	departed this life
turn up your toes	left us
drop off your perch	lost
pop your clogs	gone
	at rest
	the big sleep
	gone to the last resting place in the sky

If we do try to avoid death and dying, does that matter? If it does, how does it matter?

The implications of denying death

It could be argued that the use of euphemisms enriches our language, giving us more choice and variety of expression. And anyway, we all know what we mean. But euphemisms can cause confusion and there are times when clarity and precision in language are very important. When breaking the news of death, or the diagnosis of a terminal illness, to a relative or friend it is important to be as clear as possible. This is an issue which is fully dealt with in chapters 4 and 8. It is especially important, too, to be clear with children, who may take a more literal approach to language and have not yet absorbed some of the subtleties. To tell a child that her friend has 'lost her granny' might seem very odd to the child. Similarly, the use of 'gone' or 'gone away' does not distinguish the death of someone from a holiday or business trip. It is not only the risk of confusion in the child's mind which is cause for concern, but also the use of euphemisms which can leave the matter open to interpretation. Why has daddy 'gone' without telling me? Do I not matter? Has he perhaps 'gone away' because of something I said or did? We need to be aware that any tendency to deny death can leave children without the knowledge and understanding that they need to cope with their fears and fantasies about death and dying. We often assume that young children do not have the cognitive capacity to take in such concepts as death and dying, but research by Richard Lansdown, a psychologist at Great Ormond Street Hospital, indicates that quite young children have an understanding of the concept of death and that we should therefore always assume that they may understand much more about death than we believe they do. The inhibition about talking about death and dying is more likely to stem from our own discomfort and does not protect the child.

Denial of death has implications at the other end of the age spectrum, too. Because most deaths in Britain occur in old age it is older people who have to live with death more than any other identifiable group. They have to live with the actual deaths of their partners and peers and with the prospect of their own death, sometimes for a considerable length of time. It is much harder for older people to avoid or deny the subject of death than it is for younger adults. Studies of older people indicate that they do think about death and dying a great deal. In a study that we conducted into the attitudes of older women to their own health we found that, unlike ourselves as researchers who found it hard to bring up the topic of death and dying, the older women were not reticent and welcomed the opportunity to talk about it. Some were quite matter of fact:

Well I know I'm nearer death, you are nearer death when you get older

I shall be here until me time comes. I'm not worried when me time comes, it comes, you can't do nothing about it.

Some were quite happy to contemplate the fact of their own impending death but were aware that younger people did not like to discuss the subject. One 90-year-old widow said:

I said the other day, I'm going out as much as I can now, I say you never know when I might die. Cor, they say, shut you up! Talking like that about dying. But that is right though. I've got to be serious about that now at my age.

Others were more fearful; one said, for instance:

I fear death, I fear, will I live here and die here on my own?

There is a danger that because older people are associated with death and dying they are segregated in institutions removed from the mainstream of society and marginalised in order to make their dying unobtrusive. If society finds it hard to cope with both dying and old age, this can result in older people and younger dying people not getting the help and support they may need to face their own impending deaths and the deaths of their loved ones. Norbert Elias, writing about 'the loneliness of the dying', put it this way:

> *Closely bound up, in our day, with the greatest possible exclusion of death and dying from social life, and with the screening-off of dying people from others, from children in particular, is a peculiar embarrassment felt by the living in the presence of dying people. They often do not know what to say. The range of words available for use in this situation is relatively narrow. Feelings of embarrassment hold words back. For the dying this can be a bitter experience. While still alive, they are already deserted.*

(ELIAS 1985, P. 23)

There are many people who feel that to characterise our society as death-denying and talk of death as a 'taboo' subject is an overstatement, and that recent developements have opened up the subject. The modern hospice movement has done much to make death and dying more bearable. A quick look in the bookshops will show that there is an abundance of literature on the subject, and it has always fascinated poets and philosophers. There is even a 'natural death society' dedicated to raising people's awareness of death and the fact of their own mortality. The television has also entered the arena, with programmes such as *Merely Mortal* on Channel 4 and Martyn Lewis's *Living with Dying* on the BBC. There is also an Open University course for those who wish to study the issues. It has been pointed out, too, that as Britain is a multi-cultural society there are many people who do observe the more public forms of death and mourning rituals and hold religious beliefs, and that this has an effect on the rest of society. Britain is indeed a very complex and diverse society, and so to claim that any particular attitude to death and dying prevails is bound to be an oversimplification. However, too many people who are dying or bereaved experience avoidance, embarrassment and sometimes hostility from other people, and many people admit to these feelings.

It would be comforting to think that those who work in hospitals or other institutions which frequently encounter death and dying were somehow better than the rest of us at talking about and facing death and dying. But the evidence suggests otherwise: that, in fact, the medical and allied professions are particularly bad at dealing with death, that the whole medical enterprise is geared to preventing death, and that death represents a failure and the dying a constant reminder of that failure.

The modern hospice movement has done a lot to improve the way dying people are treated; we look at this area in more detail in chapters 3 and 5. But it is often our own fears about death and dying which inhibit us from relating to dying people and many people believe that we have to face our own fears if we are to be able to help dying and bereaved people in both a professional and a personal capacity.

Fear of death and dying

It has been said that the fear of death is universal, that it is one experience that all humans share. Many would dispute this and point out that attitudes to death and dying vary widely. Much of the difference depends on what people believe about life and death and their attitudes to mortality and immortality. Religion can provide a framework for understanding death and dying, and for many this takes the 'sting' out of death. However, some religions have in the past engendered a great deal of fear about the afterlife, with threats of hell and damnation for those who sin and do not repent before they die. Modern-day Christianity plays down the more literal depictions of heaven and hell, but in common with believers in most of the world's religions, Christians still hold some belief in an afterlife. In a multi-cultural society like Britain we need to know something about the religious traditions on which many people's beliefs about death and dying are based. This is particularly important for those in the caring professions who are likely to encounter people with very diverse views on death and dying.

Beliefs about death

Although there are different versions of Christianity, a tenet basic to all of them is that eternal life can be found through the death and resurrection of Jesus Christ. Some Christians have fairly concrete views about what constitutes eternal life and expect to be reunited with loved ones when they die. Death for them, far from being a fearful prospect, is something to look forward to, unless of course the loved ones were not so well loved. However, most Christian belief is ambiguous about the precise nature of life after death, and most present-day Christians do not believe in a resurrection of the body but rather that the spirit is not extinguished. Muslim faith is based on the teachings of the Qur'an, which states that life and death belong to God and people die according to God's will. Life is a time of probation and death therefore has to be accepted. Provided that a Muslim has lived according to the teachings of the Qur'an then they have nothing to fear in death. The third monotheistic religion, Judaism, does not specifically teach about an afterlife, but continuity of the Jewish people with God is a central tenet of Judaism alongside the importance of acts on earth.

The other great world religions, Buddhism, Hinduism and Sikhism, all believe in some form of reincarnation. Hinduism has the most developed form of reincarnation. The main aim of life is to prepare the self to be with the God Krishna. It takes many lives to reach a state of readiness to be with Krishna and selves are reborn in human or animal form until they can free the self to be with God. Sikhs also believe in reincarnation, but they do not adhere to the caste system of Hinduism. Buddhism takes many forms and has no real sense of heaven and hell; but there is a strong belief that death does not mean extinction. Life is very much a preparation for death, and there is great belief in continuity and consequence. Members of all these religious traditions practise certain rituals surrounding death and we will discuss these in the next chapter. It must be stressed, though, that many of the beliefs and traditions have been adapted to life in Britain and adherents of all of these faiths may interpret the belief system variously. Broadly, for most religions, death is but a transition to some other state, whether that transition is direct into eternal life or whether the course is protracted through many more lives.

Does this make death less to be feared? Carl Jung, the influential philosopher, believed that it did and that human life was unbearable otherwise. He uses the analogy of a house to describe what he means:

> *When I live in a house which I know will fall about my head within the next two weeks, all my vital functions will be impaired by this thought: but if on the contrary I feel myself to be safe, I can dwell there in a normal and comfortable way. From the standpoint of psychotherapy it would therefore be desirable to think of death as only a transition – one part of a life-process whose extent and duration escape our knowledge.*

(JUNG 1938, P. 129)

Freud very much disagreed. For him, any belief in an afterlife is just as much a denial of death as is an unwillingness to think and talk about it. Humanists, a secular group, also take a similar view, believing that death is an end and that there is nothing to be feared in nothing. It is life and living which are important. Humanism focuses on the importance of human linkages and relationships. Death is the end of life, and if we live on it is only in the memory of those we have known in our lives. This could be described as a form of symbolic immortality which gives meaning to life. Many people who do not believe in a god or an afterlife feel very strongly that their memory or influence will carry on after their death. Some believe in a biological immortality, that they live on through their children and their children's children. Others see a continuity with nature and the indestructibility of matter. One 70-year-old woman felt that burial in segregated graveyards or cremations was a waste. She believed in recycling the human body:

> *I feel that a right and proper end would be to be recycled through kit-e-kat or something like that, be recycled. I feel that dropping off the food chain just because I'm human is not proper. It's not morally defensible.*

Others are more content with their creative energies continuing through their work, for example teaching, writing, art or construction.

There are many diverse and sometimes conflicting beliefs about death and immortality. For most of us death remains a mystery, and we interpret that mystery in different ways. It is important to respect the interpretations of others, which may be quite different from our own. Although much of this book focuses on the practicalities of supporting dying people and their carers, we firmly believe that it is just as important to find ways of giving emotional and spiritual support. In order to do this we need to understand something of the beliefs and attitudes of dying and bereaved people. It is particularly important for those in the caring professions to try to understand the particular beliefs of the dying and bereaved people whom they are trying to support, to grasp just what are their fears and expectations.

Even if people have come to terms with their fears of death, often another fear remains, namely fear of dying and of the manner in which they will die. This can create a deep sense of anxiety for many people, especially older people who may be living alone with little social support. This book aims to address ways in which we can make the process of dying less feared for those who are dying and those who are caring for them.

Experiencing loss

Another important aspect of the way in which people approach death and dying, their own or that of someone they value, is their reaction to loss. The experience of loss is a common life event. Some losses are trivial but irritating, like losing your umbrella. Others can be more than irritating, like losing something of value, either monetary or sentimental. Some losses can be the inevitable consequence of a change which is more positive, like moving to a bigger house. Friendly neighbours may be lost but there are other gains. But there are losses which are wholly negative, such as the loss of a needed job, or the loss of a limb or one's hearing. The losses with which we will be engaging with in this book are arguably even more devastating: the loss of a loved one or the prospect of losing one's own life. Some of the feelings associated with loss are common to most losses, but the more painful emotions are felt in relation to death and dying. A range of emotions thought to be associated with loss is listed opposite. That list includes some very uncomfortable emotions, and of course not everyone will experience all or indeed any of these when they face a significant loss. We can identify two main components to losses which hurt. One is that we miss something or someone to which we were attached; the other is that we have to make changes as a result of that loss, and we usually perceive these as changes for the worse. John Bowlby used the term 'separation anxiety' to describe the feelings we experience when we lose something to which we are attached. He believed that humans attach themselves to people and to things for security and survival; therefore when we are threatened by the loss of someone or something we value, we experience deep distress. His theories were developed initially in relation to infants and the attachments they made to their mothers. There are many problems associated with his theory in terms of child-rearing practices, but his belief that attachment behaviour is fundamental and that later attachments are modelled on those we made as infants has influenced our thinking about loss and bereavement. The implications of Bowlby's attachment theory are that people will be profoundly shocked by the loss of a loved one; they will resist accepting the reality of the loss and will seek to regain what they have lost, even if that is not very rational; and they will find it very hard to deal with the loss.

Feelings associated with loss

fearful	lonely
sad	vulnerable
numb	hurt
insecure	helpless
apprehensive	worthless
dazed	vengeful
misunderstood	distress
bewildered	grief
pain	restless
shocked	anxious
guilty	afraid
angry	unloved
panic	powerless
tired	self-pity
disorientated	disbelief
burdened	denial
alienated	unwanted
unhappy	afraid

Source: adapted from Ward and Houghton (1987).

As well as arousing 'separation anxiety', loss invariably involves change. When this is perceived as wholly negative then it adds to the distress. Peter Marris, writing at about the same time as John Bowlby, believes that we have an inbuilt inclination to predictability and a resistance to change. Not only do we attach ourselves to people and things, we also attach meaning to them, as in the phrase 'something means a lot to me'. Colin Murray Parkes developed a theory of 'psycho-social transitions' to try to understand the kinds of losses which bring about a profound change in our lives. Losses which require us to make these transitions involve us in rethinking the expectations we have of our lives and our world. He refers to these expectations as our 'assumptive worlds' which 'contain everything we assume to be true on the basis of our previous experience'. Having to change these basic assumptions and the things we take for granted is not easy and it can be very frightening and threatening. He describes what is involved in the following passage:

> *Waking in the morning, we can put on the light, get out of bed, and walk to the bathroom because we have an assumptive world that includes assumptions about the presence and layout of the doors, windows, light switches, and rooms in our home, and assumptions about parts of the body that we must use in turning the light on, getting out of bed, walking across the floor, etc. If as a result of some life event we lose a limb, go blind, lose our memory, move to a new house, or have the electricity cut off, we must revise our assumptive world in order to cope with the numerous discrepancies that arise.*

(PARKES 1988, P. 56)

If we lose a spouse or partner, parent or child, or anyone to whom we are attached our assumptive world can be shattered. Everything that is familiar becomes unfamiliar; we no longer have confidence that our assumptive world is safe and we no longer have that familiar person to share it with us. That is why bereavement can be so devastating and hard to cope with. If we are to support people in their grief then we need to try to understand some of the feelings that they are likely to experience. Some writers have described the process of grieving as a series of stages through which people go before they begin to rebuild their lives after a close bereavement. There are many problems attached to the use of these stages as a way of understanding bereavement, and we will address those fully when we turn to the task of supporting bereaved people in chapters 8 and 9. The stages which have been described by most writers are:

- **Shock and disbelief:** this is the initial reaction to the loss of a loved one. Numbness, bewilderment, disorientation and a loss of perspective characterise this stage. It is thought not to last for very long.

- **Pining**: this follows the initial stage of shock as the full realisation of what has happened sinks in. It is a period of intense grief and sadness which brings feelings of pining for the dead person and a lot of mixed but intense emotions such as guilt, anger, loneliness, depression and despair. The grief tends to dominate the person's life.
- **Reorganisation and reintegration**: in this stage any real hopes of recovering the loved one are given up and the bereaved person starts to adjust to a world without him or her.

Unfortunately, this progression has been interpreted rather rigidly as the stages through which all bereaved people must go, and sometimes a timescale is even attached to it. Instead of being a descriptive tool to help us to understand some of the feelings that grief may bring, it becomes a blueprint for telling a bereaved person how they should react and is used as a measure of their progress. Understandably many bereaved people have objected to their unique experience being moulded in this way and to being told how they ought to feel and behave. Others, because of religious or cultural traditions, will react in different ways which may be defined by their own specific mourning rituals. The stages are only of value if they help people to understand some of their own feelings. If they do resonate with their own experience then it can be reassuring to know that others too have felt like that. In chapters 8 and 9 we will develop these issues in relation to a range of bereavements and to the way in which bereavement counselling has developed.

The stages of grief described above are very similar to the stages which Elisabeth Kubler-Ross identified in analysing the reaction of people to the prospect of losing their own life, a loss which threatens entirely our assumptive world. Her work (Kubler-Ross 1970) is very famous and widely read and has been very influential on both lay and professional people; but it can, like the stages model of grief, be interpreted too rigidly, leading to dying people being pressurised into fitting a mould which they do not find helpful. Her model is presented in the box overleaf:

THE KUBLER-ROSS MODEL

First, **denial** – This can't be happening to me, there must be some mistake, I'm going to wake up and find it's all a bad dream.

Second, **anger** – If this really is happening to me then it shouldn't be, I don't deserve it, it's somebody else's fault. Someone or something has to be blamed and raged against.

Third, **bargaining** – What deal can I do to prevent it, or at least put it off until after my granddaughter's wedding or until I have finished a particular piece of work?

Fourth, **depression** – When hope is lost and the full impact of impending death is faced. This is often the result of physical deterioration and weakness. Fear of dying may be acute and anguish, guilt, helplessness and despair take over.

Fifth, **acceptance** – in this final stage all struggles are given up and there is a letting-go of the hold on life. This brings relief, but it is not necessarily a happy stage and may be completely devoid of feelings.

Although Elisabeth Kubler-Ross never intended it to be so, her model has for some people become the 'correct' way to die. Many critics have pointed out that people do not invariably go through those stages and certainly not in one particular order; they may oscillate between two or more, and may never experience anger, denial, bargaining or depression. But most controversy has arisen over the last stage, which suggests that people eventually accept their fate. Some may do so, some may not; others may appear to do so in order not to upset their relatives and friends. Does Kubler-Ross's model represent the ideal way to die? Is it the way to a 'good death'? Is there any such thing as a 'good death'? What are we trying to do when we aim to 'ease' the dying of others? The next chapter looks at the idea of a 'good death' and the different ways that this is perceived in relation to a range of factors including age, gender, socio-economic conditions, cultural traditions and the type of death.

2

Is there a 'good death'?

Reaching the stage of acceptance in the Kubler-Ross model, after experiencing the more uncomfortable emotions of denial, anger, bargaining and depression, might seem a desirable way to end one's life. Accepting that death is inevitable gives dying people the opportunity to say and do all the things that they have left undone, to make preparations for their funeral, if that is what they would like to do, and to make arrangements for those they leave behind. It allows for the saying of goodbyes and the affirming of affections. 'Last words' take on a special significance. We would probably all like to say something memorable and meaningful as we depart. But does acceptance make the death 'good' for the dying, or is it just more comforting for those left behind? Some, like the poet Dylan Thomas, think that death should be 'raged' against, while, in the verse quoted at the beginning of this book, John Keats's vision 'to cease upon the midnight with no pain' is a much more tranquil affair. Many would agree that they would prefer a pain-free death, but not all would want this if it were at the expense of consciousness. Then there are certain religions and cultures which lay down rituals and customs which are necessary to achieve a 'good death'. The concept of a 'good death' is not one-dimensional and we need to be aware of the diversity of aspirations which are held. What I may consider a 'good death' may be quite different from your concept and the very idea that death can ever be 'good' is anathema to some people, although most of us would agree that some deaths are better than others. In this chapter we are going to look at certain criteria which are frequently used to determine what makes for a 'good death'. This will lay the foundations for an exploration of the practical implications for professional carers of helping people to realise their own hopes of a 'good death', which will be drawn out in later chapters.

Age at death

The health of a society is usually measured in terms of life expectancy and infant mortality. Low infant mortality and increased longevity are considered good things, signs of progress. We operate with notions of 'timely' and 'untimely' deaths. The death of a child is seen as a tragedy, a waste of a life, whereas we are more comfortable with the death of an old person, especially if that death comes at the end of a fulfilling as well as a long life. Eric Erikson, a developmental psychologist who put forward a theory of personality development, suggested that the aim of the last stage of life was to have reached a state of 'ego integrity' where the individual has found meaning in life as it comes to its end. Many older people reminisce about their past lives; this process of 'life renew', as Butler has called it, is thought to be therapeutic in that it enables older people to reflect on their past and make sense of it before they die. They may even reconstruct events and try to reintegrate past conflicts; as Butler writes: 'Such reorganisation of past experience may provide a more valid picture, giving new and significant meanings to one's life; it may also prepare one for death, mitigating one's fears' (1963, p. 68).

Being 'ready' for death has two dimensions. One is to have found meaning, like this 70-year-old woman quoted by Jane Shapiro:

> *I have lived life fully and enjoyed it greatly, which makes it easier to consider bowing out than if you felt that you have missed out on a lot.*

> (SHAPIRO 1989, P. 556)

The other dimension is to be prepared, which is not easy, as this older woman described to Rory Williams who was researching attitudes of older people to illness and death:

> *There's always a reticence in dealing with that. They think that it's a foreboding, that it hastens it on, but it doesn't. A cousin of Hamish's lost his mother and his sister within a very short time and*

sadly he went himself within a couple of years, the same trouble. But I always remember what he said: when he was left alone he said he was going to prepare, have everything in order, prepare for going and continue living. And he did so, and forgot about it; did all his preparations, forgot about it and then went on living.

(WILLIAMS 1990, P. 97)

Older people need the opportunity to talk openly about their thoughts and feelings about death and dying. If others are embarrassed about the subject and deny the reality of death for them they will find it harder to reach this state of preparedness. Being able to talk openly about death and dying also allows people to discuss where ideally they would prefer to die, which is another aspect of what makes for a 'good death'.

Place of death

Although well over a half of all deaths take place in hospitals and only just under a quarter occur at home, dying at home is what most people say they would prefer. Home represents the ideal place to die for many people. It is familiar, and they will be able to see family and friends. Perhaps we all cherish the idea that we will die surrounded by loved ones in the comfort of our own homes, fading serenely away after making our peace with the world. Reality rarely matches our ideals, however, and dying at home can mean a lot of distress for relatives and friends. Depending on the cause of death our bodies will not necessarily fade quietly away. They may cease to function in various unpleasant and embarrassing ways and we may be in pain. The modern hospice movement developed in response to a perceived need to improve the quality of dying and to provide as homely an atmosphere as possible for dying people and their carers. The following case study represents some of the tensions that dying at home can bring and indicates how combining home care and hospice care can improve the quality of dying for all those involved.

THE DEATH OF SARAH

Sarah was 68 and had been a widow for four years. Two years ago it was found that she had breast cancer which was already fairly well advanced. She had a radical mastectomy and recovered well from the operation, and then had a course of radiotherapy which had not been particularly pleasant. For a year she seemed to be well and went back to living on her own. She and her husband had moved to live near to their only son when her husband had retired, but he died of a heart attack soon after they moved. Her son, John, and daughter-in-law, Margaret, had supported her well through her bereavement and her daughter-in-law had been a real source of strength through her operation. She felt that she had had more than her share of misfortune but was pinning her hopes on making a good recovery so that she could enjoy her grandchildren, especially the youngest, Jenny, who was only six years old. When secondary tumours were discovered in her ovaries she just went to pieces and could not cope on her own. Her son and daughter-in-law brought her to live with them. They were not particularly well off and lived in a three-bedroomed semi which was only just big enough for their growing family of two teenage boys in addition to Jenny. However, they turned the sitting-room into a bedroom for Sarah and made her feel welcome. Initially it was because Sarah was so depressed that they had brought her to their home but as the weeks went by she became much frailer and they were worried about how they would cope as she deteriorated. Their own GP suggested that a home-care nurse from the local hospice should call and advise them on how best to cope and this they found very helpful. She also arranged for Sarah to go to the hospice day centre on the two days a week that Margaret worked. Even so, things became very strained. The boys were resentful that they had to be quiet most of the time and that they had no privacy. Jenny, the little girl, found it hard to understand why her granny, who used to be full of fun, was now so frail. John felt guilty that it was his mother that was the cause of such disharmony and started to stay late at work rather than face the situation at home. Margaret had always got on well with her mother-in-law but they had not been very close and she worried about having to carry out the more intimate tasks of caring which obviously would soon be necessary. Also, she felt angry with the rest of the family for not being very helpful.

Sarah was aware of the tensions surrounding her and she too was worried about her own dying and the extra burden this would bring. When she was at the hospice day centre she asked to see the social worker and told her all her anxieties, how she was worried about the effect she was having on the household and how she was especially sad that her once good relationship with her granddaughter was now strained. She was relieved when the social worker talked openly about planning for her death, telling her that either she could come into the hospice when she felt ready or they could explore intensive domiciliary support at home so that the burdens would not all fall on Margaret. Because of the disruption in the household, Sarah felt she would prefer to come into the hospice, with which she was now quite familiar and where she felt at ease. This decision was a great relief to her and took away the uncertainty about what was going to happen. It was important that it was her decision and she felt quite strengthened by it.

Margaret was at first appalled that her mother-in-law would not die at home and she immediately felt guilty that they had not been making her feel welcome. She rang the hospice to say that they would prefer Sarah to stay at home but would be glad of more nursing help. The social worker pointed out to her that Sarah had made the decision and that it was important that she was able to have some control in the manner of her dying. She reassured Margaret that they would not be excluded from her care and that in the hospice they could make sure that Sarah had as pain-free a death as possible. Margaret calmed down and was secretly rather relieved; but she was worried that John would not agree. In fact, he too was relieved as he was finding it very hard to face the idea of his mother dying at home – he had been trying to shut the prospect out of his mind and had been avoiding his mother as a result. The thought that there was relief available and that their resources would not be stretched beyond endurance lifted a great cloud from the household. The social worker also suggested that Jenny should come to the day centre with Sarah where she could meet other children whose relatives were facing death. Margaret and John had not been able to tell Jenny that granny was dying and were so relieved when the social worker said that she would talk to her. The hospice had large scrapbooks that they used with young children to get them to draw their feelings about dying, and gradually Jenny and Sarah became good friends again. Margaret and John took to sitting with Sarah in the evenings instead of busying themselves with other things.

Sarah became frailer; she was very tired and often felt nauseous. When her GP called she asked him if he thought she was near the end and he said that perhaps it would be a good time to go into the hospice. She was there for three weeks before she died. Margaret and John visited her each day and were with her when she died.

Although Sarah did not die at home, she was able to make choices and have some control over her own dying. The hospice enabled her to prepare for her own death and spend the little time she had left in tranquillity with her family rather than in a state of tension and resentment. She in fact spent more time with her son in the last month of her life than she had for many years. She was able to die with dignity, knowing that she had taken control over her own affairs. For Margaret and John, the last few weeks enabled them to relax and give Sarah the support she needed, and they felt sure that this was what Sarah wanted. They felt that she had excellent care in the hospice which they would not have been able to give to her at home, and they were also able to be with her when she died. They were not left, as some relatives are, thinking 'if only' – we had spent more time with her, made her feel more wanted, not argued about her within earshot – or about any number of ways in which they could have behaved differently.

Cultural factors

In medical terms, no heroic attempts were made to prolong Sarah's life and her death was fairly quick. Others might want to fight death and try any type of therapy which might give them extra time, even if that time is quite stressful. A 'good medical death' could be described as one where every possible technological or chemotherapeutic avenue is explored. Ethical conflicts arise when life is artificially prolonged, and these conflicts will be discussed at the end of this chapter. Some people only feel able to accept death when they are sure that everything possible has been done, that the medical profession has done its best; on the other hand, others resent the intrusion into what they consider a natural process. It is very difficult to 'let someone die' in a hospital setting and death is only considered good when it has been resisted. This sometimes has consequences for other aspects of dying, such as religious and cultural needs; these are explored in the next case study.

THE DEATH OF RAMJIT

Ramjit Sunil was only 53 when he had his first heart attack. It was about 3.00 in the afternoon and he was dispensing in his chemist's shop when he felt a searing pain in his chest. He knew immediately that it was serious and called his wife, Narawi, who was serving in the shop, to come and help him. She was very frightened by his pallor and called an ambulance. It came very promptly and the crew gently carried Ramjit, who was quite a big man, into the ambulance. Narawi went into the ambulance and they were quickly on their way, with flashing lights and sirens, to the nearest casualty department. En route the ambulance crew were reassuring and said they would have him in good hands as soon as possible. Meanwhile they monitored his blood pressure, gave him oxygen and calmed the situation down. When they arrived at the hospital, the casualty officer examined Ramjit and confirmed that he had suffered a heart attack; within half an hour he was in the coronary care unit wired up to a monitor and receiving treatment to deal with the attack. While this was going on Narawi was taken into the relatives' room of the coronary care unit, where an auxiliary nurse gave her a cup of tea and told her that they had all the latest technology in the unit and that he wouldn't get better care anywhere. She asked Narawi if she would like to telephone anyone and Narawi realised that she had not let her son know, nor had she put the burglar alarm on in the shop, so she was grateful for this opportunity. The doctor came in to talk to Narawi and told her that her husband had suffered quite a severe heart attack but that they now had everything under control. He would need to stay in the unit for about two weeks, depending on his progress, but there was no reason why he shouldn't make a good recovery. She went to see him on the unit and although she was a little appalled at all the wires stuck on to him she was relieved to see that he looked more his usual self. Ramjit was obviously relieved to be in the unit and somewhere where he felt secure.

Everything seemed to progress well, and after about four days the doctors decided Ramjit was well enough to go on to the adjoining ward, where he would stay under observation for another week. Narawi, who did not drive, and her son visited every evening after the shop was shut, when Ramjit's brother could bring them to the hospital. They had managed to get a locum dispenser and Narawi ran the shop. She was able to convince Ramjit that the shop would manage without him for a good month so that he could rest thoroughly when he came home.

Within two days of being transferred to the ward Ramjit suffered another massive coronary. He was rushed back into intensive care and all the resuscitation techniques were tried, well beyond reasonable hope. He died at about 6.30 in the evening as Narawi was on her way to visit him. She was met by the sister as she entered the ward and ushered into sister's office. There the doctor told her the dreadful news. She was distraught. The doctor told her that they had done everything in their power to save him and tried to comfort her by saying that it had been a quick death and that Ramjit did not suffer, that he probably had not even known that he was dying. All this was of no comfort to Narawi, in fact it had the reverse effect. Her husband had died alone, without his family around him, and they had not been able to carry out any of their religious rituals to ensure him a good passage into the next life. She would never be able to forgive herself. Her son was of little help because these traditions were not so important to him.

In medical terms this had been a 'good death'. Everything possible had been done, the best medical expertise and technology had been brought to bear. Some would say that the fact that Ramjit did not know he was dying and was looking forward to going home, that he had not suffered prolonged pain and had not had to experience a long illness, was reason to call this a 'good death'. On the other hand, if age is used as a criterion for determining a good death then Ramjit had died an untimely death. But in terms of his religion, and for Narawi, it was not a 'good death'.

The Sunils were followers of the Hindu religion and it is very important for Hindus that certain practices are carried out when someone dies. The family should be around the bedside not only to give comfort and support but also to read from the sacred Hindu texts. The lips of a dying Hindu person should be wetted with Ganges water and a sacred leaf should be placed in the mouth. A person should die, preferably, lying on the floor, with the name of God being recited. Many religious and cultural practices are difficult to carry out in a hospital setting but if staff are at least aware of the special needs of the minority ethnic groups that make up British society then every effort can be made to try to allow for them.

Sikh rituals surrounding death are very similar to those of the Hindu religion, with family and friends reciting from the Sikh holy books and holy Amrit water in the mouth. Again the name of God should be recited at the actual time of death. A 'good' Muslim death is also one where family and friends gather round and recite from the Qur'an. At the point of death the Declaration of Faith or Shahada is said, and if possible the dying person should face towards Mecca. Buddhists require peace and quiet as they die to allow for meditation, perhaps aided by a monk or religious teacher chanting passages from the scriptures. They prefer to die in a fully conscious and calm state of mind, and so it is important that any medication should not induce oblivion. Many Christians may wish to receive communion or mass before they die, and a minister or priest might be called in. Similarly, a rabbi may be called in to join in prayer and facilitate the recitation of the confession on the deathbed of a Jewish person, who should not be left alone as he or she dies. All those present should recite psalms and the Declaration of Faith or Shema when the death actually occurs. As well as these practices which are to be carried out as death approaches, most religions have certain ways of dealing with the body and well-defined mourning rituals, which will be discussed in later chapters. Carrying out these rituals is essential if death is to be considered 'good' for those who subscribe to a particular faith.

Any sudden and unexpected death like Ramjit's makes it almost impossible to carry out religious or cultural rituals, and so in that sense might be thought to be a bad death. Sudden and unexpected deaths are also difficult for those left behind, and researchers have shown that this is one of the factors that can make grief more difficult to deal with. Guilt and recriminations are common when there has not been the opportunity to make up for a harsh word spoken or a kindness left undone. Added to this, there is often a heightened sense of unreality when someone you may have been talking to just a few hours previously no longer exists, and this can lead to feelings of great vulnerablility when nothing seems reliable or predictable. When the sudden and unexpected death is also considered 'untimely' then it is even more difficult to deal with. Conversely, there is also a frequently held view that a 'good' way to die is without warning – 'she went in her sleep and mercifully didn't know anything about it'. What may be good for the dying person can be bad for those bereaved. However, people who are suddenly bereaved are often anxious to find out if their loved one 'knew much about it', was conscious or, more importantly, in pain. Dying in great pain is a real fear for many people and having to watch someone die in pain is possibly worse. Are anticipated deaths better than sudden deaths, and if so for whom?

Anticipatory grief

Deaths which are anticipated are those which come after a known and extended terminal illness. Unlike sudden deaths, there is forewarning. People who know they are dying from a terminal illness can put their affairs in order, make their farewells and prepare themselves for death, and they can arrange for whatever religious or cultural ritual they subscribe to. Some even organise their own funerals and leave written or other types of mementoes for loved ones or posterity. This all seems very rational and suggests that the dying person has reached the stage of acceptance which Kubler-Ross identified. Reality may not be so tidy. If someone is angry about their death or is deeply depressed by the thought of it they are not likely to be in the frame of mind to take control of their affairs quite so rationally. They may be extremely difficult to help and make it very hard for either formal or informal carers. There is a danger that when we talk of a good death we are in fact referring to a well-behaved death, which makes it easier for the carers but not necessarily for the dying person.

Is a death which is anticipated easier on the bereaved? The term 'anticipatory grief' has been used to denote the way in which those who have forewarning of the death of a loved one will begin to grieve even before the death, and it has been suggested that this might lessen the impact of the bereavement on them when death actually occurs. They do have the opportunity to get used to the idea, to get over the shock, and they have the opportunity to do everything they can to care for the dying person and to say and do the things they would like to do. But they may also have to care for a loved one through a great deal of physical and emotional pain which will put an immense burden on their own resources. Carers often talk of lasting 'scars on the memory'. The process of dying may be protracted over months and sometimes years. They may, through sheer exhaustion, say and do many things they might subsequently regret and have to face their eventual grief much depleted both emotionally and physically. Caring for someone with Alzheimer's Disease can be particularly harrowing when the whole person seems to disintegrate and scarcely resemble the person with whom the carer has shared a life for perhaps over half a century. The way in which an anticipated death is experienced will depend on many factors, not least the help and support available from professional carers.

It is hard to be categorical about what constitutes a 'good death'. Is it easier to identify what constitutes a bad death? Dying in poverty and pain, or isolated and forgotten, might be most people's notion of a 'bad death'. Sadly, this is not an uncommon experience. The late David Widgery, a GP who practised in the East End of London, documents many deaths which seem quite shocking. An old person who has fallen out of bed and died alone on the floor because they could not get help; a man who had drunk himself to death and been left rotting for days surrounded by a pile of empties. No doubt we could document many more such horror stories. What many of such cases indicate is the impact of socio-economic circumstances on the quality of dying. Older people make up one of the most impoverished groups in our society and when this is compounded with loneliness and isolation then the quality of their dying can be less than good.

Violent deaths also fall into the category of a 'bad death'. Road accidents, plane crashes and other mass disasters are events we fear both for ourselves and for those we care about. Murder, although statistically rare, is usually much publicised and fills us with a deep sense of dread. Suicide is almost always considered a 'bad death' for those who were close to the person, although there are arguments for claiming that some suicides are rational and represent the person's wishes, indicating that they took control of their own situation. These are contentious issues which are not unrelated to those raised by the question of euthanasia and the use of living wills.

Euthanasia

The actual word 'euthanasia' has its roots in the Greek language and literally means 'good death'. Many people use the term 'mercy killing'. The issues implied by the term 'euthanasia' are the subject of a great deal of debate and controversy involving both legal and ethical issues. It is a complicated debate because the concept of euthanasia is not unitary. The central feature of euthanasia is that the life of an individual is foreshortened not by the individual him/herself, as in the case of suicide, but by the intervention of another person. There are two pairs of main types: active and passive, voluntary and involuntary, with the possibility of many permutations:

- active euthanasia occurs when a person's life is ended by the action of another, for instance by a lethal injection of morphine;
- passive euthanasia occurs when a person's life is ended because of the omission of a life-saving act, such as the withdrawal of a ventilating machine when the person is in a coma and cannot breathe on their own;
- voluntary euthanasia occurs when individuals indicate or have

indicated that they wish for their life to be ended in certain circumstances;

- involuntary euthanasia occurs when a person is unable to indicate their wishes and it is decided either by the courts or by the medical profession that the life should not be prolonged.

No form of euthanasia is legal in Britain, nor indeed in any other country, although the laws in the Netherlands are interpreted more liberally. It is accepted in Holland that a doctor who 'assists' death at the specific request of the patient will not be punished if certain criteria are fulfilled. These criteria are that:

- the request from the patient must be explicit and made freely and in an informed way;
- all other treatment options must have been explored and the suffering of the dying person be beyond palliation;
- the doctor must have consulted with another physician.

Source: K260 Death and Dying, Open University 1993

In Britain euthanasia is an offence under section 2 of the Suicide Act 1961 and carries a maximum sentence of 14 years, but professional people are less likely to be convicted than lay persons and until the conviction of Dr Cox in 1992 no British doctor had ever been found guilty. The issue has become acute, because technologically life can now be prolonged after all the vital functions have ceased. The concept of a social death has been applied to persons who are not conscious and are not capable of sustaining life without the aid of technology. The issues surrounding euthanasia have had a high profile in the media recently because of the cases which have come before the courts.

Public opinion seems to support the legalisation of euthanasia, with surveys consistently showing about 75% in favour. The Institute of Medical Ethics argues that the present situation is untenable in so far as it reflects a tacit agreement to overlook the actions of those doctors who do assist the deaths of their patients. The IME claim that this puts doctors in an invidious position and also leaves patients without any choice or control over their own fate. One of the problems is that people who are artificially kept alive are not able to make choices about their treatment. Decisions are made about what the doctor and/or relatives think they would want. To help deal with this dilemma the 'living will' or 'advanced directive' has been promoted in parts of America and has some strong advocates in this country. A 'living will' is a written document made when the individual is of sound mind which states what they would choose to be done should they be in a coma or vegetative state or terminally ill and not in full possession of their faculties, for instance if they were in an advanced state of dementia. The 'living will' can state whether the individual wishes to be resuscitated in the event of a cardiac arrest, whether they wish to be artificially fed or ventilated or otherwise kept alive for instance with the use of antibiotics. In other words, it only makes decisions about passive euthanasia, and cannot request a lethal injection to be given. However, a 'living will' still has no legal status in this country.

Advocates of 'living wills' and of any move towards liberalising the laws relating to euthanasia claim that the motivation is to relieve suffering and to give people more choice and control over the manner of their own death. Opponents argue that it could erode the collective will to improve the quality of dying and believe that good palliative care can take much of the pain and distress out of dying. There are many people whose religious convictions prohibit the practice of euthanasia. Hindus and Sikhs believe that life should not be ended artificially and for Muslims the belief that death is entirely a matter of God's will prohibits human intervention in controlling the time of death. However, the distinction between active and passive euthanasia is not always clear, and rigorous resuscitation could also be interpreted as interfering with God's will. Buddhists are more concerned with the intention behind the acts and would want to be sure that the motivation is compassion. Catholics are also concerned with intention, and the 'doctrine of double effect' allows for the administration of a sedative or pain reliever which may cause death if the main intention is to relieve pain and suffering.

The issue of euthanasia is not clear-cut and opinions can be sharply divided. This itself illustrates the diversity of attitudes and beliefs about death and dying and the different views that people have about what they think constitutes a good death and how they would prefer to die. Professional carers will have their own beliefs and attitudes. It is always important to be aware of this diversity if we are to respond to the feelings of dying people and their carers.

3

How are dying people cared for?

Over the past hundred years many changes have taken place in the way dying people are cared for. Clearly where people die and who cares for them are major factors in determining the quality of dying. In this chapter we will explore these two factors which are shown diagrammatically in figure 3.1.

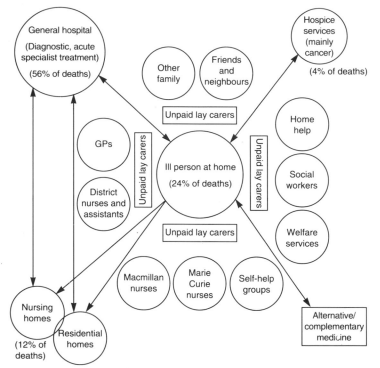

Figure 3.1 Main sources of help for dying people
SOURCE: FIELD AND JAMES (1993, P. 9)

Where does the caring of dying people take place?

Explanations for why so many people die in hospital nowadays must take into account wider social changes such as smaller family units, as well as the medicalisation of health care and the professionalisation of death. The ageing population in Britain is a crucial factor – people live longer and consequently many older people, especially women, live alone unsupported by carers. Indeed, of all deaths in 1987 44% of women and 20% of men lived alone. Where there are carers, they are often old and in poor health themselves and unable to look after the dying person adequately. If the lack of family carers is compounded by poor local services for dying people and hence inadequate pain relief, hospitalisation is often the only alternative. Although the factors are interrelated, we will first look in more detail at the implications of where people die before exploring who cares for dying people.

Paradoxically, although most actual deaths take place in hospital, most of the long-term care of dying people takes place in their own homes or in residential settings such as nursing homes or homes for older people. Cartwright and Seale's (1990) comparative studies of people dying in 1969 and 1987 has demonstrated a decrease over the period in the number of days spent in hospital over the last year of life. People now tend to go into hospital for a short time just before they die. Hospital beds are scarce resources, reflecting current hospital admission practice and policy as well as increased numbers living in homes for older people. As we shall see later, dying people move among a number of settings depending on both their physical requirements and their social needs. Factors determining the location of caring include the nature and predicted process of the illness and local provision of services, as well as the dying person's own social, housing and financial circumstances.

Deaths in hospital

When people die in hospital they are either in the accident and emergency department or on an acute ward. Following a road traffic accident, a stroke or a heart attack, people are usually seen first in accident and emergency. Accident and emergency (A&E) departments tend to be very busy, with lots of people rushing about, and many people waiting to be seen. Priority for attention depends on the perceived seriousness of the condition, and the place in the queue. Dying on a stretcher or in a cubicle in the A&E department can be a lonely, frightening experience. Pressure of work may mean that those staffing the department do not have the time to sit and comfort a dying person, as the following case study illustrates.

--- **A DEATH IN A&E** ---

Joan was rushed to hospital by her husband Tony on the advice of the GP. She suddenly developed a very high fever and had problems breathing following a flu-like illness. On arrival at A&E she was quite calm and being an unassuming quiet person was happy to take her place in the queue waiting to be seen by the doctor. Tony requested that she be put in a cubicle and covered with a blanket as she was feverish. Hours elapsed before anyone saw them again; there had been an accident in the local factory which absorbed the attention of most of the staff. Tony noticed that Joan seemed to be having great difficulty breathing and called a nurse. He wanted to call their children but felt he could not leave Joan alone. Although the nurse reassured him that they would not have to wait much longer to see a doctor, both Tony and Joan became progressively more anxious. The nurse recognised that Joan was really in a critical condition and alerted the casualty officer, who felt however that he could not leave another patient with severe burns. Joan was starting to cry for help in between gasping for breath and Tony became desperate. By the time the casualty officer arrived Joan was moribund; she died shortly afterwards.

Most fit and well people do not suddenly develop a serious condition from which they die quickly, so this case study must be seen as illustrating the worst situation that may occur, where a dying person does not receive adequate medical attention and is not comforted or reassured. Joan's husband, Tony, did not want to leave her alone because of her terror of suffocating. Consequently, when Joan died, they were alone, without having notified their children, and felt frightened and isolated. The nurse was frustrated that despite her attempts to get medical help, the casualty officer was unable to leave another seriously ill patient and give Joan the medical attention she required. Providing appropriate attention in this environment is often difficult and patients, relatives and staff may all feel compromised. Chapter 8 will explore the implications for bereaved people of seeing their relatives or friends dying in such an 'unfriendly' environment.

The decision to admit a dying person to a hospital ward is usually made because a crisis of care has developed or the person is experiencing acute symptoms. Many studies have demonstrated the inadequacies of terminal care provided in hospitals. These suggest that dying people may suffer discomfort without sufficient pain relief and are often isolated in hospital wards by nursing and medical staff who share a curative model of medicine, viewing death as a failure. The 'blame' may be apportioned to the medical establishment, largely hospital-based, which may not adequately address the range of needs of dying people, for example their need for information. A conspiracy of silence surrounding dying people is described; this suggests that it is felt that telling dying people what is wrong with them may create unnecessary and unwanted disturbances and might even hasten death. On the contrary, according to this view, a dying person should be encouraged to retain hope of recovery. Being open with dying people may be seen as counterproductive for all concerned.

Dying in hospital is associated with a number of disadvantages for all concerned – the dying person, their relatives and friends, the professional carers and the hospital itself. The way in which hospitals are organised limits the amount of control and flexibility available to patients. For example, rapid turnover of junior staff can be confusing and distressing for dying people, particularly if they experience difficulties with communication. For the dying person, admission to hospital means removal from familiar people and surroundings, and often the necessity to cede control and conform to institutional norms. Institutionalisation in itself can be an unsettling experience. Relatives may be unable to visit regularly, because of a variety of restrictions or because they themselves are not very robust.

Dying people are usually spread throughout the hospital and placed on acute as well as chronic wards. Policies regarding specialist terminal care wards in hospitals vary; some hospitals have associated continuing care units, others feel that designated terminal care wards are seen as areas of no hope and should be avoided. The distribution of dying people depends on the availability of beds as well as the patient's complaint. The management of death and dying will vary according to the type of ward; even the designation of the ward may not determine the staff's attitude towards terminal care. For example, one cancer ward may concentrate on heroic curative treatments and hence dying people may not be top priority; another ward may pride itself on pain control and provide an excellent all-round service, including spiritual and emotional care. The same variations may apply to geriatric wards. Acute medical and surgical wards are unlikely to provide optimal care for dying people simply because of the demands of acutely ill patients.

Caring for someone who is dying on an acute ward can be difficult for nurses who are burdened with large numbers of dependent, needy patients. Assigning appropriate staff time to provide intensive physical and emotional support can create an imbalance and have implications for ward management. Hence dying patients are often neglected. The priorities of hospitals are usually geared towards tending acutely ill, potentially curable patients – and, increasingly, meeting financial objectives. Dying patients are an uncomfortable reminder of the limitations of medicine, and may be time-consuming.

Yet dying in hospital is not uniformly an unpleasant experience. Our study of nurses working with dying patients in a teaching hospital demonstrated the awareness on the part of ward staff of the negative aspects of hospital wards, such as the regimentation and lack of privacy. They endeavoured to make up for these drawbacks by being very attentive to patients, attempting to create a home-like atmosphere and sharing their own lives with patients. For example, nurses told patients about their social disappointments and successes and described their off-duty activities. Nurses facilitated easy access for relatives and, where appropriate, maintained limited contact with them after the patient had died, attending the funeral and sending a Christmas card. Nurses became attached to patients and were distressed when they took a turn for the worse or died. However, they learned where and how to express their feelings, so as not to upset other people on the ward. There will be further discussion of these issues in chapter 5.

Over the past thirty years the nursing profession has endeavoured to develop its own discrete philosophy and practices, separate from those of medicine. Emphasis is increasingly placed on the whole person and nursing assessments, rather than specific instructions from medical colleagues. Caring for dying people, even within the predominantly 'curative' atmosphere of a hospital, is viewed by many nurses as 'proper nursing' as it incorporates many aspects of good nursing care. However, enabling dying people and their relatives to manage the last period in their own style is often hard in a hospital environment. The twin problems of caring for dying people in hospitals and for their relatives after death has occurred have been the subject of several guidelines published over the past ten years to suggest ways in which hospital staff of all categories (including managers) can improve the status of dying people and facilitate arrangements for bereaved relatives.

Nursing and residential care for older people

There are substantial numbers of 'forgotten' older people in the UK, especially women, who spend their twilight years in residential care and die on average within two years of admission. For these residents there are constant losses and changes from the moment of admission. Many enter these homes as a relatively autonomous 'client' or 'resident' and then rapidly undergo what may be a traumatic transition to the role of 'patient' with all its implications.

Evidence is sketchy regarding how many residents actually die in the homes, and how many are sent to hospital when they become acutely ill. Residential care for older people and nursing homes are maintained by a range of local authority, voluntary and private organisations. The nature of the licence held by the establishment determines the extent to which nursing care can be carried out; hence some facilities have no choice but to admit a resident to hospital once death approaches, depriving the resident of the opportunity to die in familiar surroundings.

Deaths occur frequently in residential care, with an annual 'turnover' of up to a third. Despite this, training for residential staff tends to focus on rehabilitation and improving quality of life, and rather avoids subjects related to preparing staff and residents for death. Jennifer Hockey (1990) studied death and dying in residential homes, and states that these homes are often seen as places where one goes to deteriorate and then die. She noted that the philosophy practised in residential care separated out living from dying. This is contrary to the philosophy of the hospice and palliative care movements, which integrate dying with living.

Indeed, some studies which have investigated the quality of dying in residential care suggest that death is kept hidden and even denied. Dying people are moved out of the main thoroughfares of the home and after death the bodies simply disappear. Residential workers have described how bodies are removed at night, through the back door, and no one mentions the deceased thereafter. Homes are often understaffed, and even where care staff would like to provide one-to-one care for a terminally ill resident they are often subject to the same kinds of work and time constraints as hospital nurses and may feel frustrated by their inability to provide quality care.

Residents rarely have the opportunity to participate in caring for their dying friends; sometimes they are not even invited to attend funerals or hold their own remembrance services. Even where they feel the loss acutely, this is not necessarily recognised by others. However, some homes now acknowledge the depth of relationships between residents and facilitate residents' participation in the terminal care of a dying person, enabling them to sit with the dying person and then with the body after death. Although this is an example of good practice, not all older people want to be so close to death, and staff need to be sensitive to the wishes of individual people.

Hospices

The hospice movement as we know it in the UK today was founded in the 1960s by Dame Cecily Saunders with the establishment of St Christopher's in south London. However, several institutions calling themselves hospices already existed in the UK from the beginning of the twentieth century. The impetus for founding a modern hospice movement arose out of a number of factors, including demographic changes such as increased longevity and smaller households (as discussed above), and in response to a public recognition that dying people were suffering unnecessarily. Most of the media attention, then as now, was focused on cancer deaths, which were perceived to be excruciatingly painful and drawn-out.

The first hospices set out to alleviate the emotional suffering of dying people as a result of isolation, and to acknowledge that it was possible to attain a tolerable quality of life while dying. In addition, a major thrust was to develop a coherent programme of pain relief and symptom control for dying people which enabled them to remain alert and as pain-free as possible, and avoided unnecessary admissions to hospital. Considerable research into ways of alleviating physical pain and other symptoms was spearheaded by hospices and developed by drug companies. New concepts in pain control have been developed; these include acknowledging that pharmacological preparations often have both physical and psychological side-effects which need to be anticipated and, if necessary, treated.

The hospice movement also drew attention to the variety of needs faced by dying people, including, for example, the recognition that there are other kinds of pain as well as the physical which merit attention – spiritual, emotional and practical issues also cause dying people pain. It also appreciated that not only the dying person has needs to be addressed: other people in their networks (family, neighbours) who are striving to care for them also require support of many different kinds.

There are over 600 organisations providing hospice-type care in 1994; these include in-patient units – voluntary, charitable and NHS-funded (with a variety of names, such as 'continuing care units'); home care symptom control teams operating out of free-standing hospices, hospital trusts, NHS hospitals and other health settings; day-care and night-sitter services. In addition many NHS facilities have access to palliative care specialists.

Most hospice services in the UK were established by local communities or charities, often by relatives of deceased persons who benefited or might have benefited from hospice facilities. With no nationally co-ordinated strategy for planning the siting of hospices according to demographic needs, provision is very patchy, with certain areas having excessive provision and a dearth of services elsewhere. Hospice facilities vary considerably in many respects, not only in the number of beds available but also in terms of whether they have access to inpatient treatment such as radiotherapy and surgery, day-care provision or facilities for respite beds to enable informal carers to take a break. The composition and structure of 'hospice' staffing and administration also varies. Some organisations strive to operate a non-hierarchical institution. Hospice philosophy is based on the concept of multi-disciplinary teamwork, which responds to the needs of dying people and their networks. Most inpatient units have a medical director (to satisfy prescription laws) and nursing and domestic staff. The spiritual needs of dying people are often catered for by chaplains from several denominations. Other employees or consultants may include social workers, physiotherapists, aromatherapists and counsellors, as well as (usually) a large band of volunteers who may work in the inpatient unit or provide support for people at home. To plug some of the many gaps in provision, Cancer Relief Macmillan Fund has placed Macmillan nurses throughout the country, and Marie Curie Cancer Care provides community nurses to support primary health workers in areas of low hospice provision with specialist advice (see below).

Admission to hospices is often restricted to those predicted to die within six months; a hospice's charter may limit admission to patients suffering from cancer, or from other specific illnesses such as AIDS. Hospice provision for adults dying of degenerative complaints such as motor neurone disease or multiple sclerosis is poor; children's hospices have a larger proportion of sufferers from neurodegenerative disorders and concentrate particularly on providing respite facilities.

Home care

Although a relatively small number of people (under 25%) actually die in their own homes, 90% of the care of dying people in the last year of their lives takes place in their own homes prior to, or between, admissions to hospital or hospice (Neale 1993). This care is usually provided by unpaid carers who are often relatives or friends of the dying person. Most deaths at home result from long-term illnesses, characterised by inadequately controlled symptoms.

Dying at home is the stated preference of a number of groups on which research has focused, including some cancer patients studied. The advantages are obvious: home is familiar and comfortable, and the dying person can feel secure; control of the dying process can be vested in the dying person and the relatives. However, the experience of dying at home may not always be as positive as these images may suggest. Many people have no carers, and even when they do families and domestic partnerships may vary in terms of their capacity to meet the dying person's social, emotional and practical needs. Symptom control can be difficult to manage, especially if lay carers are not regularly supported by professionals expert in pain relief. Coping with the physical aspects can be exhausting, as can providing 24-hour nursing care with little respite. Yet resorting to admission to an institution can create feelings of guilt and remorse for lay carers who want to keep the dying person at home.

Maintaining at home people with conditions such as motor neurone disease or multiple sclerosis may pose more practical obstacles than is the case with someone dying of certain kinds of cancer. The more physically dependent the dying person, the more difficult it is to provide adequate care without the availability of at least two strong adults. Arranging toileting, and changing the position of a non-responsive body, can be humiliating and distressing for both dying person and carer. Nonetheless, institutionalisation does not necessarily resolve the humiliation of the dying person, and indeed insensitive treatment by professional carers can additionally burden the relative with guilt.

The impact of health and social welfare policy

The implications of the changing nature of health service provision, the government's impetus to reduce bed occupation in hospitals and the push towards community care are all likely to result in increasing numbers of people receiving terminal care in the community, whether with relatives, in their own homes or in hospices, nursing homes or residential care, regardless of individual preferences. In addition, policy changes related to GP contracts and purchaser/provider deals developed by the Conservative government of the 1990s may aggravate the distress of some dying people and their informal carers. For example, if a general practice feels that a particular continuing care unit does not offer value for money and prefers the idea of caring for dying people at home, a patient in this practice may not be able to gain admission to a non-fee-paying hospice. Alternatively, as death becomes imminent some dying people and their carers may become concerned about remaining at home and prefer the idea of hospitalisation; in this situation, the knowledge that bed availability is extremely limited and that their general practitioner does not have a contract with a local hospital may create greater uncertainty and distress.

Who does the caring?

Please turn back to the beginning of this chapter and look at figure 3.1 – the main sources of help for terminally ill people. You will note that the first line of workers are the unpaid informal or lay carers. These may be the spouse, other relatives, neighbours or friends of the dying person. In addition there are several layers of other carers, other less closely involved relatives and friends as well as many professional and voluntary services.

The nature of the care provided, the combination of different types of carers and the site of care will depend on many factors and may be constantly changing. Care in its broadest sense will be responsive to changes in the medical condition as well as the preferences of the dying person. As the disease progresses some problems may be resolved while others emerge. Often the ill person will want to remain at home and maintain control and independence. However, when the dying person cannot manage alone, a key carer needs to be identified who can remain involved as long as possible. The choice of key carer will depend on the networks already in place. By default the burden usually falls on a locally available willing and able family member (often a spouse or a daughter), on reasonable terms with the dying person and the professional carers, to co-ordinate care and liaise with professionals and informal carers. In an ideal world the key carer is supported by others, both lay and professional, but their skills may be limited or subject to time pressures and they may be unable to stay the course. Additional skills may be required as the circumstances change. Selecting appropriate carers, and maintaining an open mind about introducing new carers with different skills, can be taxing and create conflict.

When someone is dying in an institution, the professional staff of that institution will usually provide the care required themselves or bring in appropriate support from outside. Health care in the community is usually co-ordinated through the primary health team led by the GP. Regardless of the nature of the practice, the GP is assisted by a number of paramedical staff; larger, fund-holding practices may employ several disciplines. District nurses provide the hands-on nursing care for ill people at home and, depending on their own pressures of work, are often willing to bath patients, turn them and administer medication. Where available, specialist nurses, such as Macmillan nurses or those working in hospice home care teams, provide a domiciliary service to advise district nurses, GPs and lay carers on a range of issues. They will be aware of the most recent developments in palliative care, know how to assemble and run a syringe pump (see chapter 6) and recommend appropriate aids. The specialist nurses will have information about other networks who provide professional services to dying people.

In addition, local authority and health services provide a number of domiciliary as well as residential services. Provision varies among geographical areas, and depends on local resources. Domiciliary services include meals on wheels and home carers (home helps) who might shop, cook and occasionally clean for a dying person; this service is usually paid for by the client according to their means. Residential services available depend on local and personal resources; the private sector has grown substantially during the years of Conservative government and caters for the very infirm as well as dying people. Where little statutory provision exists, some people are forced to sell or mortgage their homes in order to pay for private care.

Planning care

Who does the planning and how it is done will inevitably be subject to policies and local support constraints. Planning care will depend not only on available support but also on the preferences and opinions of dying people themselves. Some people have fixed ideas which will conflict with the experience or views of professional palliative carers. Deciding which informal and professional carers should be involved and where the dying person should be located can be very difficult. To illustrate some of these practical and social caring dilemmas we present below some case studies. Much of the literature concerned with death and dying focuses on people dying of cancer, because cancer deaths can be relatively rapid and are sometimes predictable, whereas the dying process in chronic ailments such as cardiovascular degeneration is less easily defined. Our case studies drawn from clinical and research experience include an older woman dying from cardiac failure as well as a middle-aged man with motor neurone disease. Consider the questions below as you read the following case studies:

1 What are the practical problems to be addressed?
2 Are the professionals providing a good service?
3 Might the situation have worked better with a different plan?
4 In which ways might the quality of dying have been improved?

——— AN OLDER DEPENDENT WOMAN ———

Eighty-seven-year-old Agatha Crown suffered from congestive cardiac failure. Now that she could no longer cope alone at home her daughter, Monica, also a widow, who had just retired, suggested that she came to live with her in her own home. As her children were adult she could accommodate her mother. This worked well for several months until Agatha could no longer manage the stairs and Monica felt guilty each time she left the house. Initially Monica had not anticipated the deterioration to occur in this way, expecting her mother to have to be hospitalised or else simply to slip away in her sleep. Additionally she was concerned that she would not be able to fulfil her promise to babysit for her son and daughter-in-law, who lived some distance away, for three weeks whilst they went on holiday.

Monica contacted her GP, who agreed to visit Agatha to assess the situation. She found Agatha bedridden, suffering from acute breathlessness and covered with bedsores. Apparently Agatha resisted Monica's attempts to wash her and turn her at night. The room was dank and dusty. Dr Gray told Agatha that she felt she needed more active care and that two alternatives existed: either she agreed to visits from district nurses or else she would have to be admitted to hospital or a residential home for short- or long-term care. Agatha agreed to the former as long as Dr Gray herself visited regularly.

The local district nurse supervisor assessed Agatha and frankly explained to Monica that their workload was such that Agatha could only be visited twice a week. She suggested that Monica contact social services for home carers and the local branch of Age Concern who might be able to provide Agatha with voluntary sitters. Monica set all these agencies in motion, and found the voluntary sitting service particularly helpful as she feared to leave her mother at all. The new arrangements continued until the time arrived for Monica to babysit her grandchildren, when – very reluctantly – Agatha agreed to respite care in the geriatric ward of the local hospital, under whose care she had been for some time. Monica felt relieved to leave her mother in 'good hands'.

However, on admission to the hospital Agatha deteriorated rapidly and died within three days of admission. Monica felt she'd let her mother down, knowing that she wanted to die 'at home', and that she had promised her that the hospital admission was only a temporary measure. She's been finding it very difficult to come to terms with her mother's death.

Sorting out the practical issues of care for Agatha seemed to be relatively easy as long as she could remain in Monica's home with good support from outside agencies. Both she and Monica were satisfied with the quality of her care until Monica needed the respite to look after her grandchildren. Moving Agatha disorientated her and Monica, having tried hard to do the best for her, was left with the knowledge that Agatha's last days were unhappy.

AN INCAPACITATED MAN

Matthew Clark was a 45-year-old divorced man who lived with Jill and her two children. The relationship was unstable and Jill had for some time considered leaving him because of his violent tantrums. Matthew had a good job as a builder but noticed difficulties with co-ordination. He visited the doctor who referred him to a neurologist. It emerged that he had an untreatable condition known as motor neurone disease and would require constant care for the remaining three to five years of his life. On hearing the diagnosis Jill moved out with her family and Matthew was devastated. He managed for several months, but eventually became unable to swallow or use his upper limbs. He was entirely alone; his neighbours kept their distance and even his GP was not particularly interested or knowledgable about MND. Matthew was determined not to be admitted to hospital, nor to a hospice, and decided to try to co-ordinate his own care using available services.

The greatest source of help came from the MND Association. They suggested the kinds of assistance Matthew needed immediately and predicted the course of the illness. Their local representative visited Matthew and volunteered to talk to the GP on his behalf. The consultation led to several referrals – to local social services for meals on wheels and a home carer to prepare meals and do some shopping, to a speech therapist to help Matthew with eating and swallowing, and to the local district nurse team. All but the home care service, which was means tested, were free.

For some weeks Matthew felt he could manage with the help of these services. As his verbal skills deteriorated telephonic contact became progressively more difficult and the speech therapist suggested calling in the local hospice team for advice. They recommended that, as Matthew did not have family or active neighbours, the only solution was for him to be admitted to some institution. Matthew was firmly against this idea and insisted on carrying on as before. This meant one short visit per day from one of the carers, all of whom knew where to leave the key for the next caller. By now Matthew was restricted to the special chair provided by the MND Association. He died of a choking spasm, alone in his chair, to be found the following day by a district nurse.

Matthew's problems were many and his condition was rapidly deteriorating, which made planning care difficult. Because he lacked informal carers, the hospice team felt the best solution was admission but Matthew was keen to remain at home. His death was miserable, and had provision been made for 24-hour cover, he might not have died alone. However, his wish was to remain independent.

A CHILD

Eight-year-old Tracey lived with her single mother and her 15-year-old brother. As a toddler she had had a brain tumour removed, the stress of which contributed to her father's departure from the family. Her mother, Carol, worked full-time as a doctor's receptionist and when Tracey's tumour recurred was in a quandary about what to do. The children's hospital responsible for Tracey's care felt that Tracey would be best kept at home during the terminal phase as Tracey's numerous previous admissions had made her hospital-phobic. However, as Tracey lived some distance from the hospital, their symptom control team could not visit regularly although they were happy to offer telephone advice. As Tracey became weaker, Carol became frantic. How could she arrange her work and yet ensure that Tracey received adequate care?

The health visitor in Carol's surgery suggested that Carol should take a leave of absence to look after Tracey during the terminal stage. Carol's employers agreed and suggested that a local children's charity could be approached for a grant to help them financially. Tracey became progressively more dependent, lost her sight and became unable to feed or toilet herself. Carol nursed her day and night and became exhausted. By this stage the district nurses were coming in twice daily to wash and turn Tracey and they noticed that Carol was at breaking point. They suggested that hospitalisation was the best solution. Carol was determined that Tracey should die in her own bed and through her surgery network contacted the Marie Curie Foundation for night-sitters so that she should get rest. Despite her difficulties in communicating, it became clear that Tracey was in intractable pain, and the children's hospital home care team came to assess this. They set up a syringe driver, instructed Carol on its use and advised the GP on dosage and sedation. It took some time for both Carol and Tracey to adjust to the 'box on her chest' and to administer the medication in the right dosages frequently enough to enable Tracey to have short periods pain-free. She died peacefully in her own bed, with her mother beside her. Despite the financial sacrifices Carol made, she felt after Tracey's death that she had done all she could to make Tracey feel safe and secure. Some years after Tracey's death she founded a local charity to provide mothers of dying children with respite care through an organisation of voluntary sitters.

Like Matthew, Tracey's condition deteriorated and care plans needed to respond to change as it occurred. The professionals, guided by Tracey's mother, were able to provide sensitive support to both of them. In retrospect Carol feels that Tracey received the love and concern that she needed during her terminal phase.

A YOUNG MOTHER

Vicky was a 33-year-old mother of four children ranging in age from 12 years to 18 months old. Shortly after her youngest was born she was diagnosed with breast cancer. Following a mastectomy and radio- and chemotherapy she had a short period of remission after which she collapsed in the supermarket from secondary tumours in the brain. She was rushed to the local hospital.

Since her initial diagnosis Vicky's mother, who lived locally, had taken the primary responsibility for running the household, Vicky's husband being away frequently on business. Her mother managed the children and the household admirably, but found the concept of Vicky's likely death intolerable, Vicky being her only child. Vicky's response to this anxiety was to reject her mother, which caused further distress.

Vicky's discomfort increased and she was constantly plagued with pain and headaches. Tom, Vicky's husband, found her mother intrusive and decided to take a leave of absence from work once Vicky was discharged home. He found this unsatisfactory and returned to work, having arranged daily help from a nursing agency. Despite pleadings from neighbours and friends to involve the local hospice team, Tom and Vicky were determined that she would win her fight over the cancer. Their consultant, whom they saw privately, concurred with their stance, assuring them that Vicky was curable. In the meantime, Vicky tried to live as normal a life as possible; she could not drive, being forbidden to do so in her condition, but attempted to undertake her normal housework and cooking tasks.

The older children started playing up; Tom and Vicky rejected the counsellor recommended by the school. Vicky's condition deteriorated further and the nursing agency could not manage with her at home without input from specialist terminal care teams. Tom refused to allow the hospice to 'interfere', the nursing agency walked out, and Vicky was admitted to an acute ward after several fits. She died there, alone and frightened, still believing that she would be cured.

Vicky was determined not to give in to her illness and to live her life as normal. This meant that it was difficult to introduce professional help to enable her to maximise the time she had left with the minimum of pain. Her family's determination to deny the severity of her illness contributed to a poor quality of dying, in a strange environment with unfamiliar carers.

A RETIRED MAN

Brian Davey was a 68-year-old retired bank clerk who lived with his wife in their own home. Ten years ago Brian developed cancer of the colon, for which he received surgery and was fitted with a colostomy. About a year ago, the cancer recurred in the liver and in the lymph glands and Brian became weak and unable to manage alone at home. His wife, Mavis, who still worked in the bank, felt concerned about him being alone all day, particularly as he was no longer able to prepare his own meals and attend to his colostomy bag. She called their GP who came to see them at home. The GP explained to Brian that he was not likely to recover from his cancer and discussed alternative caring plans with the couple. The outcome of this visit was referral to the district nursing services and to the local hospice.

The hospice home care team visited Brian and Mavis to assess how they could help. Three members of the team came: a doctor, a nurse and the social worker. The doctor and nurse asked Brian to describe his symptoms and promised to discuss changing his medication with the GP. The team suggested that the district nurse come each evening to help Brian wash, and that he should visit the hospice day care facility to see whether he would like to attend on a regular basis. Although resistant at first, Brian recognised that Mavis worried about him being alone at home. He also found the pain frightening and would feel reassured by regular contact with medical and nursing personnel.

Brian was impressed with the hospice, found the staff helpful and attentive and enjoyed participating in some of their activities. In addition, the hospice doctor was available to discuss some of his medical problems and advise his

GP on adjusting his analgesia. The new system having worked for a few months, the hospice social worker suggested that Brian be admitted to the hospice for a week's respite care to enable Mavis to take a well-earned break with their children in Scotland. Despite Brian's initial reluctance he enjoyed the different environment, the opportunity to participate in many diverse activities and the attention provided by the staff. When Mavis returned they reinstituted the previous systems until Brian's condition deteriorated and he became bedridden.

Mavis took early retirement to care for Brian; the district nurses increased their visits, and the hospice arranged for voluntary day-sitters as well as Marie Curie night-sitters to enable Mavis to sleep. When they could no longer manage Brian's pain at home, Brian agreed to be admitted once again to the hospice. He was familiar with most of the staff and felt safe and secure in that environment. Their children came down from Scotland to visit, and he died with the minimum of pain, surrounded by his family.

Subsequent to his death, the hospice staff remained in touch with Mavis, who regularly attends their bereavement coffee groups. She hopes that in the future the hospice will allow her to volunteer as a home-sitter.

Planning Brian's care seemed effortless through his lengthy association with the hospice. As he faced each hurdle a solution could be found by the collaborative team of Brian himself, his wife Mavis and the hospice workers. All were responsive to his changing needs and moving him to the hospice for his last few days seemed a natural progression.

In each of the cases outlined here, the practical problems to be addressed differed. The site of care needs to be responsive to the individual's circumstances and needs. For example, Agatha could not manage in her home and had to move somewhere; luckily her daughter could initially care for her. Thus, for some dying people, there may be no option but to move out of their homes. Even where lifts are available they might be inaccessible for wheelchairs. For those living in houses, or split-level flats, the lack of a downstairs toilet or sleeping facilities might make caring difficult. Sometimes the local authority can be persuaded to make building alterations to accommodate a toilet, rails or a chairlift or to provide wheelchair access, but these alterations take some time and often immediate action is required.

Hospitalisation is often a last-minute decision made in crisis conditions, as it was for Agatha and Vicky. It was unlikely that either of these women felt safe or familiar in a busy acute ward. In some instances, real alternatives exist and choices can be considered in advance. For example, a hospice place might have been found for Matthew, as well as for Vicky, had either of them been willing to contemplate this earlier. Had the management been different in both these cases, the dying person could have become familiar with hospice staff as well as the actual building through day-care visits or respite care and it is unlikely that either would have died alone. Had the GP been more involved, too, the outcome might have differed. GPs are in a pivotal position and can discuss alternatives with their patients. This approach can often influence the decisions of dying people. If they have already become familiar with local hospice provision, that last admission could be a more pleasant experience, rather than a snap decision to deal with intractable pain or unresolved difficulties in providing care.

It is not always possible to facilitate people's wish to remain at home as well as providing appropriate pain control, symptom relief and excellent care. You will have noted that in the case studies given here, only Tracey might be said to have had a good quality of dying at home. Matthew, on the contrary, fought to stay at home, but could not receive adequate care. Had he been a cancer sufferer, and a symptom control team had been involved, his death at home might have been more controlled and less traumatic. Clearly it is difficult and unethical for professionals to persuade unwilling clients to accept services. In addition, financial constraints also limit the kinds of services professionals are able to provide and hence they are less likely to try to persuade unwilling clients to accept services when there are other clients actually asking for their resources.

These case studies illustrate how the constantly changing realities for dying people require sensitive responses from their carers. The next chapter will explore in some detail the centrality of good communication between dying people and all who look after them.

4

Communicating with dying people

An impetus for the development of the hospice and palliative care movement was the perception that people dying in hospital were often isolated, neglected and frightened. In particular, it appeared that the psychological impact of impending death was ignored. Many dying people were unaware of, but anxious about, their diagnoses and prognoses, and some people may have wanted this information to influence the course of events.

Telling someone that he or she has a serious, life-shortening and possibly painful illness or discussing their future, or even their current situation, is not easy. It requires skill and sensitivity to find out what someone wants to know; it is also difficult to decide how and by whom this information should be transmitted. However, the barriers to communication are rarely insurmountable.

The ways in which information is transmitted to and received by the sick person and their networks affect these relationships. Obviously the most important interaction is how the crucial information relating to the nature of the illness, whether it is treatable and how, and the likely outcome, is imparted.

Before looking in detail at how to communicate with dying people it is important to understand people's responses to imminent death.

Psychological responses to dying

The first indication that life is likely to be foreshortened can be devastating, particularly when it is unexpected. As discussed in chapter 1, Elisabeth Kubler-Ross in her pioneering studies of dying people identified five psychological stages to dying. These have been interpreted as a sequence starting with denial, followed by anger, bargaining, and depression, and ending with acceptance. Other practitioners and researchers have debated this pattern and provided a more comprehensive list of common psychological responses including shock, disbelief, fear, hope, isolation, envy, anxiety and confusion. These may appear in combination or separately, and may happen once or more frequently, in any order.

Robert Buckman identifies three phases which may incorporate some of the above reactions. In the first phase the person faced with the terminal diagnosis expresses shock and disbelief, which may affect normal functioning. Gradually they recover from the shock and enter the second phase, where the physical decline affects their lifestyle. As they approach death the final phase is entered. Several responses are common in the second and third phases – for example, fears may include those of pain, the dying process and treatment as well as of death. As we saw in chapter 1, fears can be influenced by religious belief, particularly about the prospects of life after death. More mundane fears include concern about losing control over their own lives, as well as being rejected by their circles.

Despair and depression can occur in all three phases. Despair can be seen as losing hope (Buckman 1988) or a response to receiving bad news. Depression, on the other hand, can be a realistic response to losing one's future and has a number of physical manifestations, such as insomnia, loss of appetite, weepiness and self-centredness. These may be alleviated by anti-depressants, and it may be helpful for the dying person to be assessed by a psychiatrist. Psychological responses to the prospect of death are seen by many as important, yet these reactions are rarely elicited in consultations with dying people. Both dying people and physicians tend to focus consultations on physical problems, seeing emotional and social issues as divorced from the illness. This can result in the neglect of emotional factors and lead to subsequent distress and serious difficulties.

Severe psychological reactions to dying are often seen as psycho-pathological; this label can be stigmatising and damaging in many ways. Some reactions can result from physiological involvement as a result of malignant spread to the brain and some dying people might require sedation to reduce anxiety and control paranoid behaviour.

Disclosure of information

Telling a person that he or she is likely to die from an incurable illness is one of the most difficult things a health worker ever has to do. Regardless of one's experience, personal inner strength or even knowledge of the individual patient, it is hard to know how to pitch the conversation. Everyone reacts differently to this news, and sometimes these reactions may come as a surprise to patients themselves as well as to their closest friends and relatives. Hence predicting someone's reaction is often impossible. Experienced and sensitive physicians acknowledge that sometimes they get it wrong, and this can have implications for their long-term relationships with the dying person and the family.

Traditionally, information about diagnosis is given to the senior medical person responsible for a patient's care. That physician then decides whether further investigations are required and what, if anything, to tell the sick person and/or the family. 'Disclosure' is the term used to denote the transmission of information about the diagnosis, prognosis and ultimate outcome of the illness.

Depending on the philosophy of the person disclosing the information, and/or the constraints imposed upon that person by the philosophy or policies of the workplace, the information disclosed can range from the full available facts to deliberate inaccuracies.

The following case study illustrates some features of bad practice, particularly that the increased tendency to disclose is not necessarily accompanied by appropriate sensitivity on the part of the discloser.

———— DISCLOSURE MISHANDLED ————

Michael was a schoolteacher aged 33, married with two small children. He noticed that he was having difficulty controlling the chalk on the blackboard and arranged a consultation with his GP, who immediately referred him to a neurologist. Meanwhile Michael's father mentioned the problem to his neighbour, a physician, who told him that the condition was likely to be serious. Between them they agreed that there was no point in alerting Michael or Janet until the tests proved something conclusively.

Having undergone numerous tests, the neurologist contacted Michael for a consultation and suggested that Janet be present. They brought their children along, not anticipating bad news. No one else was present at the consultation. The neurologist sat them down, told them bluntly that Michael had motor neurone disease, that there was no cure and that he was sorry. Michael and Janet were stunned and found themselves unable to think clearly. They recall very little said by the neurologist after that but are certain that he made no suggestions about how they should proceed, how long Michael could work, how the disease would develop or who could help.

For both Janet and Michael the way in which this consultation was handled destroyed their faith in the neurologist as a person who could provide some emotional if not practical support. They left with the sensation that he wanted them out of his consulting room as quickly as possible, to avoid further questioning. They feel aggrieved that they were not given leaflets or information describing the organisations which provide advice to MND sufferers and their families.

Breaking bad news or disclosing information should be seen as a continuing dialogue between a dying person and his/her carers rather than a one-off occasion. At the initial interview, when the diagnosis is first disclosed, all the relevant information regarding treatment options may not be available and further meetings should be scheduled. The chronological process may thus be as follows:

- disclosing the diagnosis, projecting the prognosis;
- depicting the likely process of the disease/condition;
- explaining treatment alternatives and the accompanying side-effects;
- sketching the symptoms most likely to develop and the implications for normal functioning;
- outlining the reasons for altering or abandoning treatment plans;
- informing dying people that the terminal phase has been reached and discussing ways in which the problems can be addressed.

Even covering just two of these aspects could include giving information as well as discussing decisions to be taken. Research evidence demonstrates that most people absorb less than 50% of details disclosed to them during consultations; this fact needs to be considered when bombarding someone with new information. When Michael learned that he suffered from motor neurone disease the shock probably prevented him from absorbing more details at the time; he might have valued a suggestion of a follow-up appointment or a referral to another expert.

How should information be disclosed, by whom and where?

First of all, the dying person must be allowed to signal whether any information is wanted. With the increasing tendency to disclose details of the condition comes inevitably the problem faced when dying people give clear signals that they do not want information and prefer not to know, believing that everything will be all right. Their right to control the information they receive must be respected, and they should not be forced to embark on conversations against their will, regardless of current thinking that it's better to be told and 'know'. Some people who want the information may reject overtures inviting them to talk about their feelings, and again their desire to keep their views private must be upheld without making them feel they are rejecting offers of help. A related problem arises when relatives are determined, for a variety of reasons, to keep information away from the dying person.

Michael's experience illustrates several aspects of bad practice. In the first place, the news was broken during a routine outpatient clinic where staff time is at a premium and there is no one available to provide support. Secondly, Michael hardly knew the neurologist; although breaking bad news to a virtual stranger may be an inevitable consequence of events, sometimes this can be avoided by enlisting the co-operation of the general practitioner or another health worker familiar with the ill person. Another common illustration of poor practice is the consultant revealing details to a hospital inpatient during a ward round. A ward round is a public event observed by many onlookers, including other patients. The sick person may be left alone with this news, with no one to provide support while the ward round moves on to the next bed. Telling someone on the ward may be unavoidable if the person cannot be moved. However, it is possible to ameliorate an otherwise 'hostile' environment. For example, the structural disadvantages of being bedbound need to be acknowledged. The person may be prone, undressed (or in pyjamas) and at a lower level than the informant, who may be standing or seated on a chair. The cubicle may feel constricted, with curtains closed, and the recipient of the news may be aware that those outside can hear the discussion. This may be a disincentive from expressing feelings such as anger or distress and may discourage the dying person from asking questions – which may indeed be the hidden agenda of the informant. The imbalance in power can be reduced by a simple measure like sitting on the bed. Where the sick person is relatively mobile, disclosure could take place in a ward office. Another health worker familiar with the dying person could be present to provide reassurance and a sense of continuity.

It may be helpful to ask the dying person if someone else – maybe a key relative or a friend – could be present at the consultation when bad news has to be given. This is advantageous for both inpatient and outpatient consultations, if only for the purpose of recalling the events and sharing the experience. Sometimes doctors are willing to repeat the information on to a tape, so that all the information does not need to be consigned to memory. Much ground is usually covered in such a consultation, and recording may be particularly useful if the key carer is not present. Where possible a follow-up consultation could be arranged so that the dying person feels supported and enabled to prepare questions and issues for the consultant.

The terms and language used need to be explicit, simple and unambiguous. Language can be misleading for dying people as the following quote about a woman with cancer shows:

> *Mrs Smith kept stopping us [the nurses] and having long conversations about what's wrong with her, but she kept repeating what the doctors had said about her having an ulcer and she kept repeating it as though she wanted us to deny or confirm this.*

Medical terminology can be mystifying, but on the other hand oversimplification can feel patronising. An assessment of the dying person's knowledge of English, what he or she already knows, as well as how much he or she will understand, needs to be made prior to the consultation, and if possible with the help of other workers familiar with the dying person.

The dying person needs to feel supported and at ease. It can help to rearrange the furniture to reduce unnecessary barriers, for example by moving a desk separating the discloser and the patient. Aids such as information packs, cassettes, leaflets, drawings or even X-rays where appropriate may simplify the information to be disclosed and aid the dying person's understanding. These can be taken away and reread at home, but the material will need to be screened for suitability, as some publications may raise rather than allay anxiety. In addition, some individuals might find such material distressing, and healthworkers need to judge whether the particular person will benefit rather than suffer from having easy access to this information. A nurse on a cancer ward comments that before handing out information she needed to check its appropriateness with the ward sister:

*I thought Martin would be interested in a booklet we have on the
ward called 'What the patient needs to know about chemotherapy'
and so I asked sister whether it would be OK to show him because
there is no reference to anything about the disease, it doesn't even
mention cancer in the booklet, just talks about treatment. I
thought it would be useful for him; he was aware of his diagnosis
but not anything further long term – I think as a student you can't
just go and hand out information before checking.*

Conversations may include encouraging the dying person to
participate in making practical decisions about such things as the site
of care or the usefulness of certain drugs. Discussions will also focus
on explaining the meaning of symptoms as well as enabling the dying
person to voice fears and anxieties about the future and problems of
coping with the present.

When planning the consultation it is useful to consider both the
immediate and long-term emotional needs of the dying person. In
some instances, even when the full facts are presented and repeatedly
reaffirmed, they may not be absorbed, as the following quote from a
nurse on the cancer ward we studied indicates:

*There was a discussion between the sisters and the doctor on the
ward a few weeks ago because some patients as a result of their
condition don't assimilate the facts and so they may say to
somebody in passing 'What's really wrong with me' as if they
haven't been told anything about their condition. In Mrs Day's
case the doctor had spoken to her for an hour the day before, and
whether her response was rejection, not being able to cope with
being ill, or that she hadn't grasped the facts despite an hour's
discussion because she has cerebral metastases was what we were
trying to work out.*

It may be helpful to include another professional at the consultation
to help answer queries, confirm what was said, provide reassurance
and, if necessary, arrange follow-up discussions to answer
subsequent questions. Who will be the appropriate person will
depend on the setting and on the networks already involved in caring

for the dying person. For example, on a hospital ward the choice of key worker would depend on the local system of nursing, and might be the primary nurse, team leader or charge nurse, or someone from another discipline. A clinic nurse or representative of the local support team might be the chosen key worker in a hospital outpatient clinic, whereas in the GP's surgery the practice nurse might fulfil this role. Whoever fulfils this role should, where possible, be familiar with the dying person.

Interpreting a dying person's questions can be complicated, as it is sometimes not clear whether the dying person actually wants to know the answers. Should one assume that the first question on this subject is an indication that the dying person really wants that information at that moment? Examples of questions being answered at face value with disastrous consequences suggest that it is necessary to clarify questions before answering them. Two student nurses on a cancer ward explain:

> *I'd ask the patient first what they actually knew about their illness, what they'd been told. And I wouldn't give them a direct answer about their diagnosis – I'd still go to a doctor, discuss it and if he said to me go and explain more fully, I would, or the two of us would go and have a chat with the patient. I think it is something that has to be discussed with somebody else, it's such a big decision whether a patient should know or not and at which point.*

> *Often they don't really want to know – they ask you but they don't want to know the answer. So you answer by going through some of the questions on the nursing admission form to the ward – what's your treatment, do you know your diagnosis, what has the doctor explained to you, do you understand it. This one patient knows he's got warts, he doesn't know he's got cancer, he thinks he's got warts.*

Hence answering a question like 'Is Dr So and So giving me all the facts?' with another question, such as 'Do *you* think that Dr So and So has given you all the facts?' can help the dying person express fears and anxieties and provide an indication of whether information is really wanted. This strategy also buys time for the person being questioned to reflect on the situation and seek advice from colleagues, as well as to check the dying person's readiness to hear the bald facts. The implicit drawbacks of stalling are that receiving a negative or equivocal response may increase the dying person's anxiety and reduce the likelihood of further questioning.

Planning the encounter

The relationship between the person imparting the information and the recipient is likely to change as a result of bad news being given. Sometimes a deterioration of the relationship is inevitable, but research and experience have demonstrated that careful planning of this interaction can reduce the damage. Buckman (1992) recommends a six-step protocol in breaking bad news:

Step 1: Getting started
Step 2: Finding out how much the patient knows
Step 3: Finding out how much the patient wants to know
Step 4: Sharing the information
Step 5: Responding to the patient's feelings
Step 6: Planning and follow-through

The above steps are self-explanatory, using the basic principles of communication skills to reduce the imbalance caused by one person possessing information about another. Buckman (1992, p. 66) particularly emphasises two components of the interview which are worth noting:

- the divulging of information, by which the professional imparts information to the patient;
- therapeutic dialogue, by which the professional listens to, hears and responds to the patient's reactions to the information.

Allowing the recipient to set the pace of the discussion – 'patient-led communication' – is a useful technique requiring some knowledge and experience of communication skills. Peter Maguire, another expert in this field, stresses the importance of establishing trust between the professional and the dying person. The professional has to earn that trust, which takes time, and can be particularly difficult where lies were previously told.

Maintaining open networks with dying people

Many people express anxieties about talking to dying people about almost any topic. The need to maintain open channels of communication has been the subject of many workshops, videotapes and books authored by Peter Maguire and Robert Buckman, to whom we have already referred. They concentrate on overcoming the obstacles to communication, some of which may be self-imposed, others of which may take the form of covert or explicit directives from other interested parties, such as health workers or relatives. Their views, although differing in some respects, share the basic premise that the best way of communicating is through open dialogue with the dying person, avoiding a power imbalance where the discloser holds all the cards. These experts believe that enabling dying people to talk about the distress they experience should alleviate it somewhat, simply through knowing that someone else is listening and interested. Avoiding discussing these issues, indeed, aggravates fears; while being close, listening and accepting the person's feelings as valid reduces the dying person's feelings of fear and shame. The key concept is to listen to people's concerns. 'Sensitive listening' (Buckman 1988) implies making oneself available to listen without imposing oneself on the dying person. Allowing dying people to express their feelings can minimise their emotional distress. Obviously hearing such pain can be difficult, and not all people are comfortable with this. Also it can be hard to judge whether the timing for talking is right.

The case study of Michael represented bad practice. We will now look at the work of Maguire and Buckman, among others, to illustrate certain aspects of good practice in communicating.

Buckman's six step protocol is particularly useful for the initial breaking of bad news and is sometimes appropriate subseqently. In all situations it is essential to plan the discussion with the dying person carefully, ensuring that the setting is comfortable and private – avoid talking in a public place. Sit at the same level, unobstructed by clutter, and maintain eye contact. However, you don't want to crowd the dying person, so don't sit too close by. You'll want to make sure that the dying person wants to talk and to indicate that you are listening carefully. Silence can be interpreted in a number of ways and needs careful observation. For example, it may mean the dying person is tired, breathless or in pain. It may also indicate that the dying person is reflecting or in need of a reassuring touch. (It is necessary to ensure that physical contact is appropriate culturally or socially.) Silences may not mean the dying person wants to stop the discussion; the reverse may be true. Sensitive observation or direct questioning could resolve the dilemma. It is advisable always to allow the dying person to set the pace. It may be very difficult for the dying person to express his/her thoughts, and interrupting could ruin the atmosphere.

Asking for clarification demonstrates that you're listening and enables you to avoid misunderstandings. Whatever you do, don't change the subject or give unsolicited advice. On the other hand, dying people may expect or want advice from a professional carer. Encouraging the person to reminisce, for example recalling coping strategies in earlier adversities, can reassure them that they have the resources to cope once again. Using humour appropriately can relieve some tension, but this needs to be culturally acceptable to both parties.

Why has talking to dying people been so problematic?

Although denying dying people and their relatives information is no longer a widespread practice, it was very common even as recently as ten years ago. The ethos of health work focused on protecting patients from information which was seen as intolerable and doctors and nurses justified withholding facts on the basis that dying people should not be deprived of 'hope' of recovery. 'Brutal' honesty would result in dying people becoming despairing and possibly disruptive. Nurses subscribed to the predominant medical beliefs that patients should be given as much information as necessary consistent with the retention of hope as well as ensuring co-operation with treatment. Where patient co-operation was necessary to ensure treatment, procedures, phrases and words were used to disguise the truth. Euphemisms, shields and other devices were employed to describe tumours or cancers. These words included lumps, ulcers, warts, borderline cells, problems, obstructions and growths. As these terms also describe some benign conditions, their use does not necessarily suggest malignancy.

During the 1960s and 1970s sociologists in the United States and Britain studied interactions between health workers and dying people. Health workers were found to plan their conversations with dying people on the basis of whether they thought the dying person knew what was wrong with them. These researchers introduced the term 'awareness contexts'. If dying people talked about the illness and prognosis openly they were seen to be in an 'open awareness context'. If both health worker and dying person knew the score but chose to pretend otherwise, they were in 'mutual pretence awareness'. The dying person would be in 'suspicion awareness' if he or she indicated suspecting the truth but did not necessarily verbalise it; or finally, in 'closed awareness' if he or she neither knew nor suspected the diagnosis or prognosis. Placing dying people in awareness contexts helped health workers make decisions about whether they could talk about the diagnosis or prognosis or other issues relating to the illness. Health workers also made predictions about when someone was likely to die and the course that this process would take; this helped them make a variety of decisions such as placing a dying person in a side ward, giving them medication and informing their relatives.

The implications for dying people of the ways in which health professionals treated them were serious. For example, when nurses talked to dying people they focused on physical tasks to avoid talking about the illness or the patients' feelings. This meant that a trusting, empathetic relationship between dying person and carer was unlikely to develop. By limiting contact to brief conversations on specific subjects, health workers avoided emotional involvement with dying people as much as possible and hence once patients were dying they were isolated. This avoidance or withdrawal from dying people was called 'distancing' and usually occurs in institutional settings, though it can also happen at home.

What were the advantages of this kind of 'detached concern' for carers? By withdrawing from the dying person carers are believed to protect themselves from painful emotional encounters. This usually occurs because health workers feel restrained from expressing feelings in their work settings; this may be explicitly stated or implicit in the work structure.

There are several explanations for the isolation of dying people. Psychoanalytic concepts suggest that distancing is a coping mechanism for dealing with anxieties related to death and dying and helps avoid emotional involvement with dying people. Distancing strategies are acquired through experience and imitation. New recruits may discover that they are discouraged from expressing their emotions by becoming attached to dying people, showing their feelings and then being reprimanded for making a fuss, not getting on with their work, and getting overinvolved with dying people and their families. This experience is likely to deter them from further involvement with dying people. 'Distancing' causes problems for those who use it – they feel overwhelmed, fearful, depressed, guilty and anxious.

Attempts to change distancing behaviour have used dynamic or behavioural psychological techniques. Courses have been implemented to educate nurses about the prognoses of cancers, pointing out, for instance, that not all are fatal and invariably painful; death and dying workshops have focused upon developing self-awareness and encouraged health workers to acknowledge and express their own fears of death and dying. Another tactic is to create an atmosphere where health workers feel enabled to express feelings. These attempts have ranged in format from multi-disciplinary consultative support groups to individual counselling for members of teams working with cancer patients and dying people.

However, contemporary nursing practice now works against the withdrawal of nurses from dying people, encouraging nurses to engage with patients and act as their advocates. Indeed, nurses may now be encouraged to become more involved with patients. 'Burnout' (see below) could result if nurses are not adequately supported. Our study of nurses working on a cancer ward demonstrated how a complex system of information control sifted through the nursing hierarchy, coupled with a very open and supportive environment for nursing staff, contributed to low incidences of both distancing and burnout. This and other similar studies reported that the dying people appeared to be well cared for and few nurses manifested the symptoms detailed above. Thus implementing structural changes can create changes in ward culture; more open and accessible management practices can facilitate more personal care for health workers as well as their patients.

If structural support is not available, health workers engaging with dying people and experiencing emotionally demanding encounters may develop symptoms of 'burnout'. Many of these symptoms resemble those experienced by health workers who distanced dying people. Other symptoms include high rates of absenteeism and low resistance to illness (such as recurrent colds, headache, stomachache, insomnia, backache, exhaustion and fatigue). Burnout can also result in drug and alcohol abuse, difficulties with decision-making and problem-solving and interpersonal problems with colleagues. Burnout is cumulative and progressive and can be viewed in stages, starting with somatic symptoms and resulting in the gradual disintegration of relationships. Hence the term describes the end result of progressive and severe occupational stress. It is particularly common where jobs include frequent interpersonal contact. Some associate burnout in health workers with the severity of the medical condition being treated. For example, some believe working with people with AIDS or cancer causes feelings of loss and increases vulnerability to burnout.

Communicating with dying people has been suggested as a source of stress for health workers which may result in dying people being isolated or healthworkers burning out. Our own study and others challenge this premise, suggesting that other aspects of work are more likely to create stress. These include division of labour within hierarchies, for example lines of responsibility and authority, inadequate staffing arrangements, working with other disciplines (particularly where professional boundaries are crossed), inadequate resources and pressure of work.

Current communication practices

With the recent changes in health service provision, consultant autonomy has been eroded, resulting in more manoeuvrability for general practitioners and health service managers. There are fewer beds in NHS hospitals with the government encouraging a free market in health care. More people are choosing to see consultants privately by subscribing to private health insurance, either individually or through their unions or workplace. As many insurance companies need detailed bills before they will meet claims, many private patients are aware of their conditions. Lawsuits for medical negligence are on the increase and the public is beginning to demand information about health. Legislation now entitles individuals to have access to their medical records.

The media has played a considerable role in informing lay people about the causes of diseases and about the treatment and care options available for people with cancer and other life-threatening conditions. This was exemplified by an article in the *Guardian* (14 September, 1993) describing how Jill Tweedie, the journalist and author, discovered that she suffered from motor neurone disease.

Alongside the personal account was an article describing different forms of the disease and related prognoses. Hence many lay people nowadays have some knowledge about the processes and outcomes of diseases. Studies investigating what lay people as well as people suffering from particular conditions would like to know have revealed that most people want full details.

Yet, despite evidence that most people want this information, many units, wards, departments and institutions still refrain from full disclosure. However, as with other contentious issues such as abortion, individual preferences often dictate the manner in which disclosure is handled. Even where policies exist, there are likely to be variations in practice. It is possible on one ward for three consultants to have completely different policies and styles regarding disclosure. This can create all sorts of difficulties for other ward staff and indeed for the patients, some of whom will know their precise diagnoses and others of whom will have been fobbed off.

With the proliferation of different kinds of consultations in a variety of settings, and the growing strength of general practitioners, factual disclosure is on the increase. As more people are party to the information, the person breaking the news could be one of a number of professionals or a relative. In some settings health workers may still be constrained from telling the truth by local policy or relatives' wishes. Some will simply disregard these instructions when they recognise that the person's distress will only be resolved by telling the truth, as the following quote from a student nurse describing a patient on a leukaemia ward suggests:

> *We had a young boy of 16 on the ward, a very intelligent Japanese boy – he was intellectually well ahead of his years and he had a bone marrow transplant and he was told he was cured completely and in fact he wasn't. He knew he wasn't. In fact the [transplant] didn't take and he had to have a second transplant. 'And he knew that because he used to say to me 'Are they being entirely honest with me?' and because he was so intelligent I used to be honest back, that was the one occasion when I was absolutely, utterly*

honest. Because the doctors used to come in and say one thing, I think they always opted on the side of optimism because they felt it would boost his morale, but I think he would have preferred more honesty. And I think he needed more advice as to what sort of side-effects, he'd get and that sort of thing. And when his side-effects became worse, he didn't understand why – the doctors were saying he was getting better so why was he getting these sort of side-effects, rashes and everything else.

This nurse's preference to be open and honest with the boy with leukaemia reflects a more widespread unhappiness among younger health workers about the concept of deceiving dying people and their relatives. With communication skills an integral part of nurses' and doctors' education, as well as central to the training of carers (as is evident in the core requirements for competencies of NVQs/SVQs), more openness and honesty are being encouraged.

If most people want information, why do some doctors persist in withholding the truth? We have already touched on rational explanations for deceiving people. Some physicians avoid disclosing information because of a very real fear of arousing patients' emotional reactions. In addition, physicians are concerned about being blamed by the patient, either because anger is often targeted at the bearer of bad tidings or because maybe the illness or deterioration of the illness is seen as someone's fault.

Specific obstacles to communication

Not all dying people are able to absorb information or respond verbally. Interactions may be impeded by the nature of the illness; for example, neurological damage can make talking impossible and cause distress. Sometimes stroke victims and people with motor neurone disease can be taught to signal their wishes and hence participate in treatment and care decisions. The person trying to communicate may be able to reduce the dying person's distress by indicating awareness of the frustration and anger felt. This may enable the dying person to retain some autonomy and sense of self as long as verbal and non-verbal communication can be understood. People with learning difficulties experience similar obstacles in communicating their feelings and the frustration, anger, grief and distress they feel needs to be acknowledged by their carers to create an atmosphere of support.

Dying people who do not speak English or whose comprehension is poor are at a particular disadvantage in a society where little consideration is given to those with a limited command of English. In addition, mistrust and even non-compliance with treatment can result where the dying person and their family belong to a different culture from the professional carers. A non-informed carer may misinterpret verbal or non-verbal cues. British professionals might be uncomfortable with noisy expressions of distress. Alternatively, someone from a culture which frowns upon expressing emotions might be regarded as repressing feelings by workers who subscribe to the western view that verbalising feelings is 'healthy'.

Cultural responses to illness and impending death vary. Some cultures, for example Hindu, encourage preparation for death. This includes giving the dying person accurate information about their impending demise as well as carrying out traditional practices before and after death. Denying Hindus this opportunity to prepare has implications for the afterlife of the dying person as well as life on earth for the mourners and can cause tremendous distress. Some cultural practices or religious beliefs may be strange or even uncomfortable for British practitioners. Adult Jehovah's Witnesses, for example, refuse treatment and may refuse a blood transfusion.

In a multi-cultural, multi-religious and multi-ethnic society such as Britain is today there are many stereotypes of different cultures. This includes assumptions and predictions about behaviour based on superficial evidence – skin colour, accents, names, etc. Education about ethnicity and regional variations in practices is rare. Hence a positive strategy is to ask dying people and their relatives, in a non-judgemental facilitative way, to describe their beliefs and practices. Respecting rather than ridiculing these views will enhance the relationships between health workers and the consumers of health services and reduce the likelihood of misunderstandings arising. Ensuring that channels of communication remain open will enable health workers to provide excellent support to dying people and their families. The ways in which this can be done will be explored in the next chapter.

5

Supporting dying people and their carers

Communicating about the illness is one important aspect of supporting someone who is dying. In this chapter we are going to explore the wider arena of supporting dying people as well as their informal and professional carers. But first we will reflect on just what we mean by support.

Many years ago I underwent training as a nurse and I remember being rather bemused by the phrase, 'reassure the patient'. This phrase was tacked on to every procedure, whether it was giving an injection or preparing someone for a major operation. What did it mean? Tell them it won't hurt, or they won't die, or that they will feel well again? I did not know any of these things, so how could I 'reassure' the patient? I think it meant much the same as 'support', a word that we use a great deal today in the caring professions and one we have already used extensively in this book. Many people have tried to break down the concept of support in order to understand exactly what it means. There seem to be three main components:

- emotional or affective support;
- cognitive or informational support;
- instrumental or practical support.

Emotional support entails involvement and intimacy. It requires warmth, affection and companionship. Giving emotional support can be very draining for professionals and they too will need supporting in these activities. Cognitive or informational support is about providing advice and information about a whole range of issues, from what to expect of the illness to where and how to get benefits.

Instrumental or practical support is fairly self-evident: it entails actually doing something like cooking a meal or helping someone get dressed.

Supporting dying people

Emotional support

Dying, for most people, is an intensely emotional affair. In previous chapters we have discussed the range of possible psychological responses to the knowledge that one is to lose one's own life. But a dying person will experience many losses before the actual death which can cause emotional distress. There may be physical losses of function – not being able to walk about freely, a loss of physical strength, the inability to perform intimate tasks for oneself with a resulting loss of dignity and privacy, a loss of physical attractiveness which might result in a loss of self-esteem. There may be social and economic losses, such as the loss of a job. Social contacts may be diminished, either because the illness restricts activity or because friends withdraw in the face of a terminal illness causing a loss of self-confidence and self-esteem. Such losses can evoke strong emotions such as anger, depression, anxiety and fear. Helping people to deal with these emotions can put a great deal of strain on carers and leave them feeling very vulnerable, but it can also be a source of deep satisfaction.

Providing emotional support to dying people is now an integral part of palliative care. The trouble is that the skills required to provide emotional care are difficult to identify and even more difficult to teach. If we could provide models of good practice it would make the task much more manageable, but individual responses to death and dying are personal and unpredictable and so any such model might work in one situation but not in another. Some generalisations are, however, possible. Qualities such as sensitivity, awareness and empathy are important in trying to understand the emotional needs of dying people. Lesley Fallowfield (1990), writing about improving the quality of dying, has suggested some more specific ways in which the needs of a dying person may be met. Her suggestions focus on three factors:

1 **Time**
Dying people need time to express their feelings, and this is related to the need for carers to listen rather than do or talk.

2 **Comfort and compassion**
Providing physical comfort enables carers to convey concern and emotional support to a dying person. There are many opportunities to provide physical comfort, from arranging pillows to simply making sure that the person is warm enough and not sitting in a draft, or alternatively not too hot with the sun streaming into the eyes. Touching and smiling can bring comfort, but it is important to make sure that this is appropriate and not an invasion of someone's privacy.

3 **Humour**
In our attempts not to be death-denying we may overwork the subject of death and dying. Dying people are also living people who will still have a sense of humour. Humour and cheerfulness can relieve depression and anxiety; again, however, sensitivity to what is appropriate, and when, is important.

Listening and observing are probably the key skills in providing emotional support to dying people. Allaying fears and anxieties, for instance, requires first that we find out what it is that people fear. They may find it hard to express their fears and anxieties, perhaps because they feel that they may be irrational. But if we are to provide the information which might put their minds at rest then they need the opportunity to express those fears.

Informational support

Broadly, there seem to be two main ways in which information could help dying people. One is to try to respond to their own queries as honestly as possible; the other is to provide them with information which might help them.

People who have a lot of experience of working with dying people have recorded some of the questions which they have been asked. Some are predictable, others represent fears and anxieties which might be thought irrational. Which of these questions would you find hard to answer?

Will –
I be in pain?
the pain get worse and worse?
I become a cabbage?
I choke?
I become paralysed?
I go mad?
I become incontinent?
I disgrace myself?
I smell?
I just waste away?
I be asleep?
I vomit?
I lose my hair?
my husband/wife still love me?
my husband/wife find me
   repulsive?

I be helpless/useless?
I pass it on to others?
I really be dead when I'm
   buried/cremated?
I know when I'm actually
   dying?
I still be able to hear you, yet
   not be able to respond?
I be alone?
How long will it take?
What will you do to my body?
Where will you put me?

The answers to some of the questions will depend on the particular disease; for instance, someone with MND is likely to become paralysed eventually, therefore acknowledging this and discussing the ways of coping with it is a positive approach to dealing with the anxiety that this can cause. Although guarantees cannot be given to questions about pain, vomiting, choking, incontinence, etc., information can be provided about modern ways of alleviating these unpleasant symptoms if they should occur. Some of the questions cannot be given a definitive answer and an honest acknowledgement that one does not know to questions such as 'Will I know when I am actually dying?' or 'How long will it take?' is better than evasion or blanket reassurance. Many of these questions do not necessarily invite answers so much as open up the possibility of discussion about something which is clearly bothering the person, for instance whether their spouse or partner will still love them or find them repulsive.

People may have questions which you cannot answer, but which may prompt you to put them in touch with others who do have relevant expertise or experience. Many self-help agencies exist today which offer help, advice and counselling to people on particular conditions. Examples include the MND Association, BACUP, the Muscular Dystrophy Group, and the Multiple Sclerosis Society. They can be particularly important, because many of their helpers have first-hand knowledge of the condition and may have experienced the same fears and anxieties.

As noted above, information about other forms of help can make an important contribution to improving the quality of dying. Alerting the person to any financial benefits to which he or she might be entitled can take away financial worries or provide extras which they would not otherwise be able to afford. Chiropody, physiotherapy or occupational therapy may be useful, as well as other community services such as home helps and meals on wheels. These services will provide more instrumental help with day-to-day living.

Instrumental support

Practical help can range from doing shopping and housework to putting in stairlifts or other aids and appliances. When providing practical support, the important issues are that it is appropriate and timely. This is illustrated by the following account from Pam Ashton who was looking after her husband, Donald.

> *I asked if they could put the shower in a place where I could use the controls without any problem. I didn't want to get soaked*

every time I went under. It ended up with the shower in the wrong place so I said, 'Well that's useless, I can't use that.' We didn't have a proper chair to take him outside in so it was a case of from his chair or his bed into the wheel chair, out to the shower room in to a commode that they'd lent me. So he sat on the commode, washed him under the shower, took him out of there into the wheel chair, back in to the living room or the bed room which it was now, on to the other chair then we could dry him down. This was a very trying performance really because by now he was having difficulty with both legs and it was not a case of stepping from one place to the other, it was a case of shuffling round at a very slow speed – you've got to hold the wheel chair to make sure that's secure, you're trying to hold the commode so that doesn't move and you're trying to hold Donald so you need six hands not two. We overcome it, we overcome it, we laughed sometimes, sometimes we cried but we got over it. Then the occupational therapist came in and asked whether we have any problems and I said, 'Well, the sink they've put in, the wheel chair won't go under it.' So he was at a sideways angle and water was everywhere because he just couldn't get close enough to the sink. I complained about the shower and asked if we could have the shower changed which they did and I'd asked for a longer hose because the hose was about three foot long and it was OK until he sat down and I was trying to shower underneath to get the soap away and the hose wasn't long enough so I ended up going to buy a new one myself, fitted it on, so we overcame that one. Recently we've had a gentleman in to change the height of the sink but to be perfectly honest it's been a waste of time because Donald doesn't go out to the sink any more, he has a bowl on the table, I wash him all over the top, we have since about April.

Although the Ashtons were provided with the help they needed, the delay in installing the shower and its inappropriate positioning meant that it never was really any help to them. This was frustrating for them as well as being a waste of resources.

There are many ways of providing practical help to dying people, and many are concerned with alleviating their symptoms. These issues are fully addressed in the next chapter. Supporting dying people also involves supporting their informal carers. Often their concerns are the same: for instance, the shower was needed by the Ashtons both for Donald's comfort and for Pam's convenience. But sometimes informal carers have separate support needs.

Supporting informal carers

Like the dying person, their relatives and other informal carers may also have emotional, practical and financial problems which arise as a result of the illness.

The needs of informal carers

Where the dying person still lives at home, cared for by a spouse, sibling or child, the burden on these carers can be considerable. As noted in chapter 3, with increasing numbers of older people living alone, the availability of local unpaid carers has decreased. Where there are elderly co-residents they themselves may be physically frail and require considerable additional physical support to enable them to continue caring for their sick relative or friend at home. There is considerable evidence of the financial hardships suffered by older people in Britain, and caring for a dying person exacerbates these. At the most basic level, additional resources require to be found for heating and transport, just to name two obvious requirements.

Even when the person who is dying is not old, the burden of caring can be compounded by other responsibilities borne by the carers; for example, many people find that they do not have sufficient flexibility in their working conditions to enable them to provide adequate care as well as fulfil their obligations at work. Other responsibilities in the domestic arena may include looking after school-age children, older relatives or other dependants. Where the dying person had previously contributed to the household budget the financial resources of the family will become strained and additional resources will need to be found to cover basic costs such as food, rent or mortgage, let alone additional costs relating to the sick person's specific needs.

While the dying person is still relatively self-caring and independent, and the carer can leave the home, the carer may still have the opportunity to get away for a break. However, as the dying person becomes more dependent, the carer needs immense emotional and physical resources to cope, as the following case study demonstrates. As you read this, try to identify the emotional, informational and instrumental support needs of the carer and think who might appropriately provide for these needs.

LEONARD

Leonard Clark was a 60-year-old builder who lived with his wife Denise in a council house in Humberside. His diagnosis of motor neurone disease was badly handled by the neurologist, who gave the illness its medical name rather than helping the Clarks to understand the implications. Atypically, Leonard's deterioration was rather rapid and within a few weeks of diagnosis he could no longer manage the stairs to go to the toilet. The local authority agreed to construct a bathroom on the ground floor and Denise converted the living room into a bedsitting-room.

Leonard was very anxious not to be housebound and as Denise could drive their car, they attempted to go out as much as possible, taking Leonard's wheelchair along. On the last such occasion they went to the coast to watch the waves, a favourite pastime of Leonard's. It was a bleak day and they were alone on the beach. When they returned to the car, Leonard got stuck getting in to the car. They struggled for over an hour, not succeeding in getting him either out or in. Denise was exhausted and frustrated and Leonard alternated between fury and exasperation. Eventually a passer-by helped to get Leonard into the car and they drove home in silence.

A few days later Leonard was no longer able to assist in his care at all. Denise became dependent on the twice-daily visits of her daughter, Annette, for help to wash and feed Leonard. When they attempted to help Leonard, he often resisted, and Denise found the experience humiliating and frustrating. She admitted to the GP that she often prayed for him to die quickly so that both of them could be spared the trauma and humiliation.

Denise no longer slept at night in case Leonard needed her, for he could not speak any more. Help during the night became essential, but they could not afford to pay agency staff and the MND Association advised them that they were not eligible for Marie Curie night-sitters as Leonard did not have cancer. Reluctantly Denise agreed to the suggestion of the local hospice support team that Leonard should try out hospice care, even on a respite basis. This was more difficult than they had envisaged as beds for MND sufferers are at a premium and few hospices have this facility. The local hospice was restricted to cancer patients, but another 50 miles away was prepared to take Leonard.

Leonard was extremely hostile to the idea of going in to the hospice, feeling he was being abandoned by Denise and Annette. Despite his lack of verbal skills he made his feelings clear, which exacerbated Denise's sense of guilt and misery. Denise continued to feel guilty after his admission as Leonard became progressively more depressed. He died after a fortnight in the hospice, having withdrawn from his family.

Carers like Denise can experience very mixed emotions when looking after someone who is dying. Many of the emotions experienced by dying people can also be felt by their carers and emotional support may be needed to enable them to continue with their caring. Carers often feel frustrated because they recognise that they alone cannot provide the required care. Denise felt compromised because she could not look after Leonard properly – she couldn't turn him on her own, and when he fell she couldn't lift him. She described the difficulties in helping him into and out of the car and an occasion when she was simply stuck, not being able to move him. Can you imagine her impatience and frustration, and can you imagine Leonard's feelings? She admitted this to her GP, who, if he or she could not give her the emotional support she needed, could have suggested that she might like to talk to a counsellor who could listen to her troubles. Relatives like Denise may be grieving for the losses that the dying person has experienced. Leonard had been a very able person, capable of great strength both literally and emotionally. She had looked to him for protection. Now he was unable to communicate, eat or move his limbs, yet she knew that mentally he was unchanged and wanted so badly to resume his protective role.

Carers talk about a whole range of other emotions which they might want to talk over with an empathetic listener. Sometimes the physical manifestations of the illness alter the appearance of their loved one to the extent that they may feel revulsion – for example when there is an unsightly or weeping tumour. Many carers say they begin to feel ambivalent about their dying relative – indeed, the relationship between the carer and the dying relative may have been difficult before the illness and illness may exacerbate some of the problems. Now the dying person is dependent, how can the carer desert him or her? Even where relationships are close, caring for someone who is terminally ill will entail a number of losses for the carer as well, emotional losses such as losing a future together as well as an active soulmate. Practical losses may include giving up work or reducing work commitments (and consequently suffering financial hardship), reducing or eliminating leisure activities, and restricting social contacts due to unavailability.

Carers sometimes experience some resentment towards the dying person for 'causing' these losses. Sometimes carers are torn by the ambivalence of wanting the dying person to live, yet at the same time wishing that they would get on and do their dying because their own lives are so disrupted and they too are experiencing such pain.

Informal carers may be able to give as well as receive emotional support and so might want to be in touch with others who have had similar experiences within self-help networks. Cancer counsellors and palliative care specialists, among others, are also able to provide emotional support and informal carers wanting to use these services should have access to them. In chapter 4 we noted that not all dying people want the opportunity to talk about their feelings or fears; some people would rather keep these to themselves. The same applies to relatives and other informal carers. Counsellors and self-help groups should not be imposed upon carers unless they would welcome it. Experiences of talking to other people in similar positions can be positive or negative and informal carers may want to know more about their backgrounds – for instance, do they have any religious or political affiliations which they do not share? – before agreeing to unburden themselves to strangers.

Informational support can be as helpful as emotional support. For instance, many carers find it disturbing to witness a dying person's uncharacteristic changes in mood and behaviour when these occur. Those closest to the dying person may be bewildered by their reaction. Leonard's anger was understandable, but to Denise it might have seemed unfair when she was trying so hard. Sometimes carers find that the dying person is withdrawing from relationships, and this can be viewed as rejection. Uncharacteristic emotional reactions from dying people can be ascribed to their perceptions of the illness or the fear of death, but may also result from the progress of the disease or the effects of drugs. Informational support from either a medical expert or someone who has also experienced this, such as someone from the MND Association in the case of Denise and Leonard could help to put this into perspective. For children, behavioural changes in adults can be particularly distressing, and their own behaviour might reflect the insecurity they feel when a parent behaves uncharacteristically.

Looking after a dying person can be immensely fatiguing, as it was for Denise who could never sleep soundly in case Leonard needed help – all her reactions were geared to protecting him. Although she dearly wanted to keep him at home, she recognised that she no longer had the capability to care for him. She badly needed practical or instrumental support if she was to carry on caring for him at home. She did receive some practical support from her daughter but, had she been able to have a nightsitter or respite care, she may have been able to avoid the very unhappy situation which left her feeling guilty and miserable.

Informal carers will welcome time out. Many organisations caring for dying people have lists of volunteers who will provide a sitting service to enable carers to get out. Volunteers and some statutory workers, such as home helps, may shop, cook or collect children from school to relieve the burden of the key carer.

In some instances relatives other than the key carers will require support to deal with their emotions, as the following case study illustrates.

ANDREW

Andrew was an accountant living in Manchester with his wife, Evelyn, who is a solicitor and their two young children, Joshua and Sarah. A few days before his 40th birthday Andrew complained of headaches. He went to see his GP who sent him to hospital immediately where he underwent brain surgery for a brain tumour. Part of the tumour was removed, but he haemorrhaged and was left in a persistent vegetative state. The children had not known that there was a problem until Andrew told the family he was going to see the GP about his headaches – that morning was the last occasion they saw their father up and about.

Andrew's parents lived in Bournemouth but were on holiday in Spain when this happened. They returned immediately to find Evelyn and the children extremely distressed, but trying to continue as normal. The children went to school and Evelyn went to the office. Sidney and Alice, Andrew's parents, found their daughter-in-law's attempts to maintain a 'normal' existence very uncomfortable and considerable conflict ensued. Andrew's parents spent all their waking hours at his bedside trying to elicit a response.

Eventually the tensions exploded and Evelyn asked Sidney and Alice to return home to Bournemouth and come back after Andrew had died. Andrew lived on for another two months during which time Alice became extremely distressed and depressed. Her GP referred her to a bereavement counsellor who enabled her to talk about her anger both towards Andrew for having become ill and towards Evelyn for rejecting her.

This case study illustrates that there can be numerous additional people involved with a dying person over and above those available locally. Family dynamics can be a complex network of relations, some supportive, others destructive. Some family members may feel a sense of obligation to care for the dying person or for his or her immediate family; others may do it willingly; and yet others may wish to participate but cannot or are prevented from doing so by 'closer' relatives or friends, as in the case study of Andrew. Many informal carers report that they are surprised by those in their network who abandon them, as well as those who pitch in to help.

For scattered families, the lack of opportunities to care can create distress, and relatives at a distance may also require support to deal with the problems that arise. Sometimes relatives who live far away want the opportunity to be involved in making the arrangements for care even if they cannot provide the care physically themselves. Integrating relatives at a distance into decision-making can be difficult for all concerned, but might alleviate some of the distress experienced by those far away.

Supporting professional carers

In an effort to provide support for dying people and their informal carers, the support needs of professional carers can be neglected. Professionals caring for dying people may also welcome emotional support from colleagues, or from members of other disciplines, as this quote from a sister on a cancer ward illustrates:

> *You all find your own outlets – the terminal care support team have availed themselves to me and I'm appreciative of that. I've always said I need that, I'm not afraid to say that I need a bit of support. I wouldn't be afraid to say to one of the doctors I really feel that I'm not doing terribly well and can you listen to me for a while – I feel I've made a mess of something – it usually means you have and you need to talk it through, otherwise you can run into*

problems. I think this is maybe a quality that you need to know on a cancer ward. There are stresses and to keep your sanity or whatever you don't let them build up; people on the whole are very happy to listen to you, you know, if you identify people that are obviously good listeners.

Clearly for junior staff, particularly on a hospital ward or in another hierarchical institution, expressing feelings to superiors may influence progress in the profession. We noted in chapter 4 that carers have traditionally used distancing strategies to protect their emotions or alternatively have burned out. Many organisations caring for dying people build in measures for staff support, which include group discussions or individual interviews with outside or in-house consultants. Opinion as to the value of these is divided; some carers feel that only others in the same position can truly understand, while others find talking to colleagues not helpful, preferring to choose their own confidantes from either their professional or their social networks. The following quotes illustrate a range of opinion from nurses on the same cancer ward:

If I were upset I'd talk to my parents – I was thinking about that the other night, if I had any problems I don't know anyone in the hospital that I could talk to about them. I couldn't talk to my tutor, I'd talk to my parents. In my first year I got attached to a patient who got very ill and I got very upset about it and I told the sister on the ward and her attitude was not really sympathetic, was more you shouldn't get involved, and when I left the ward she wrote a great deal about it in my report.

I'd never talk to any trained staff about my feelings. No, I don't think its the same anyway, I like to talk about it in a relaxed way where I can talk about what I'm feeling. I tend to go out and pour it all on my boyfriend or maybe like if we go to supper break we'd probably chat about what's happening on the ward with patients and you tend to come out with things that are bothering you then.

I think you have to go and talk it out with somebody – we seem to discuss things, don't we [to setmates] if anything's happened on the

*ward we get together and have a little chinwag about it. You can
go home to the rest of the set and they'll listen to you but they
don't really know who it is you're talking about.*

Not all carers find that talking about their feelings is necessarily the
most helpful outlet. For example, the nurses on the same ward as
those quoted here maintained that what they wanted was more
instrumental support, such as opportunities for leisure so that they
could forget about their professional lives. Their quest for leisure
time became an acute problem when they had other demands on
their time such as preparing for final exams. Attention to practical
issues such as staff shortages, poor equipment and poor working
conditions is extremely important to professionals if they are to
provide for the support needs of dying people. Informational
support, in the form of education and adequate training, is also
essential to professional carers.

Professional teamwork

Working within a team can often offer the best support to
professional carers in their efforts to care for dying people. The
most effective way of caring for a dying person is by establishing a
team of people which includes both informal carers and professional
workers as well as the dying person. The composition of this team
will need to be flexible and will depend on the availability of
services as well as the changing needs of the dying person and
informal carers.

The network of disciplines involved in caring for a dying person can
be vast. Roles will vary; some professionals will have transitory
contact, others will have intensive contact for a short period of time
and will withdraw when no longer needed, and the remainder will
have sustained contact with the dying person. Several medical
practitioners may be involved including the GP, physician, general
surgeon, specialist surgeon, oncologist, radiotherapist or neurologist;
different types of nurses may include specialist terminal care nurses
from the Macmillan or Marie Curie services or a support team,

district nurses, community psychiatric or geriatric nurses; there may also be other professionals involved, including social or community workers, occupational therapists, physiotherapists and radiotherapy technicians. In addition there may be volunteers assisting in independent hospices or charities, driving dying people to appointments or providing a 'sitting' service, as well as other ancillary staff, for example, home helps, domestic staff and porters.

Being part of a team, whether as recipient of the care or a care-giver, can provide a sense of being supported in a common endeavour. The team framework enables carers to discuss and debate issues and to use one another's expertise for the benefit of the dying person. In some settings, however, real or perceived differences in professional ideologies can result in conflict. For instance, nurses may disagree with doctors' decisions, as illustrated by the following comment from a nurse on a cancer ward:

> *I felt the doctors were prolonging life for the wrong reasons – and also the nurses on the whole too when they administer the drugs – I just felt they tried too hard to prolong life and that it was a discomfort to the patient – they seem to get their priorities [wrong], like, supposedly there's this thing about quality of life, as soon as you feel the quality of life is that much less, you should stop it before it deteriorates drastically, for example Mr White who died in great pain – little things like the doctors seemed to want to send the patients off for tests for their own interests, teaching interests, not perhaps for the patients' interest.*

However, most of her colleagues disagreed with her assessment, saying that 'we are very much a team on this ward'. They commented that the doctors valued their judgement, turning to them for advice about a range of issues, even to suggest effective drugs for 'their' patients. This sense of belonging to a team was identified as a reason for nurses requesting reallocation to this ward.

Regardless of setting, be it hospice, home, or hospital, team discussion should be seen as facilitative rather than conflict-generating. The wealth of experience and differing perspectives of both informal and professional carers can be used to produce imaginative and flexible solutions to care problems. The questions to be debated will be varied and complex and may include decisions about the eventual site of death, choice of key carer and which medications are appropriate. Sometimes one carer may suggest additional or alternative professional or lay help, and this may have to be negotiated among the team. For example, one carer may feel that the dying person would benefit from spiritual help such as a visit from the local clergyman. This can be a contentious issue within a family and will need to be debated and negotiated with the dying person.

The debates and disagreements that may develop regarding the best site for the care of a dying person are illustrated in the following case of an older dying person, narrated by a nurse on a palliative care team. This describes in some detail the kind of care that the person was receiving at home and why the professionals did not want to move her into a hospice:

> *Gloria is a 94-year-old woman with cancer of the breast which really is not a problem at the moment but she's suffering from dementia, which is. She was referred to us by her family some months back. She's surrounded by a lot of different family members amongst whom there is considerable conflict about where she would be best cared for. Quite a bit of pressure is coming from her grandchildren to place her in hospice care. Her breast cancer has been fairly well controlled with a recent course of radiotherapy; her major problems have been her dementia, she has been agitated and wandering about with no clothes on, the usual signs of dementia – their requests to place her in a hospice cannot be met because it's not the right place for her to be in if she's like that. It's been made clear to the family that unless there are definite signs of deterioration the hospice is not the right place for her to die. In many respects the best place for her to die is at home, the nursing environment has been set up very well by the district nurses, they go in several times a day, as well as a night nurse and 24-hour carers there. Still there is pressure from the family to have her*

admitted to a hospice. She has different days, some days she cannot swallow her medication, other days she's up and about and calm. But the situation may be changing now, she possibly has a chest infection.

My role has been to support the district nurses with the pestering of the family and to monitor Gloria's condition. I will go this afternoon with the district nurse to do a joint visit to see if Gloria is actually deteriorating. The district nurse feels that it may be unfair to move her if she is deteriorating so we may very well have to talk to the family about that. The GP is also under pressure from the family – he rang up the other day saying 'My gosh, the family are putting so much pressure on me, they're deskilling me, they've rung me up tantamount to saying I'm useless'. I spent a good half an hour on the phone with this doctor just saying, 'Look, you know, you've got the same problems as us, we're all going through the same thing.' It was actually a matter of our team supporting the GP and the whole primary care team . The family are very angry because they feel Gloria should have been in a hospice but she's actually in the ideal environment. Unfortunately if she's admitted for hospice care she'll die very quickly, she'll get disorientated, she'll be difficult to manage and I suspect her condition will deteriorate. It's certainly in her best interests to stay at home, I'm sure, and that, there's the conflict.

Clearly the views of the family are not well represented in this case. The professional carers are of one mind, preferring to keep Gloria at home; but the informal carers' perspective has not been incorporated into team decisions. What about Gloria's views? As she is no longer communicative, it can be hard to keep this dying person central to the team. Even when dying people are verbally competent their needs may be subordinated by the informal carers. So to whom can the dying person address questions or express concerns? Lines of communication need to be set up because, as we saw earlier, being bedridden can put a person at a distinct disadvantage. Even those whom they do see, for example a junior doctor, may feel inhibited through inexperience or lack of responsibility from answering the query or providing the advice the dying person wants. Hence that junior doctor needs to know that there is someone available with the experience and confidence that he or she lacks.

The next chapter deals with symptom control and pain relief and will illustrate how co-ordination between team members and consultation with the dying person can indeed result in a better quality of life while dying for the dying person and a sense of achievement for those who are trying to facilitate this.

6

Symptom control and pain relief

As we have already noted, the impetus to improve care for dying people was partly generated by a belief that dying people were suffering unnecessary pain and discomfort. Hence a central focus of the palliative care and hospice movements became the development of a scientific approach to pain relief, coupled with a psycho-social perspective to identify the interaction between different kinds of pain – physical, spiritual, psychological and emotional.

Palliative care, the specialism directed towards meeting the needs of dying people, emerged out of the hospice movement with a multi-disciplinary approach. The SMAC/SNMAC (1992) report defines palliative care as 'active total care offered to a patient with a progressive illness and their family, when it is recognised that the illness is no longer curable, in order to concentrate on the quality of life and the alleviation of distressing symptoms'. Hence palliative care:

- regards death as the normal and expected end to life;
- values each dying person as an individual and recognises the interactions between different aspects of the illness;
- tries to provide the dying person and his or her family with as much choice, independence and control over the dying process as possible;
- neither hastens nor postpones death but provides appropriate treatment, such as relief from pain and other symptoms;
- integrates all aspects of care for the dying person – physical, practical, emotional, psychological and spiritual;
- aims to create a team of carers, keeping the dying person and

informal carers central to this process: this team will consist of professional and voluntary carers such as hospital or domiciliary medical staff and their teams, social workers, psychologists, nurses (both in inpatient units and in the community), clergy, dietitians, physiotherapists and complementary therapists, and good communication between carers is essential;

• provides expert advice as well as emotional, spiritual and practical support for those caring for the dying person, both during the illness and after death (bereavement care).

This chapter focuses on those components of palliative care which address physical symptoms – pain relief and symptom control. Other aspects of palliative care, such as emotional and spiritual support, are important themes throughout the book and will be touched on here only where relevant.

Before embarking on a discussion of palliative care it is important to remember that for some dying people, relatives and professional carers the concept of palliative care may not be acceptable, and they will strive for cure until the last moment. It can be difficult to identify who among those involved is unwilling to recognise that death is the inevitable result of the illness; however, palliative care workers are accustomed to providing advice and information even when the dying person him- or herself is not willing to recognise that curative treatment has not been successful.

The role of palliative care workers

Professionals in palliative care, regardless of their discipline, see their role as providing support and expert advice to all those who are involved in caring for the dying person. As the problems that arise during the dying process may be complex and varied, a professional from one discipline is unlikely to have the expertise and skill to address them all. Hence palliative care is characterised by a multi-disciplinary team composed of both professionals and lay people.

There is no standard palliative care team; its composition will vary and may include different mixes of professionals as well as volunteers and informal carers. Doctors and nurses from a number of settings, social workers, physiotherapists, occupational therapists and clergy may contribute to the professional element, while the non-professional members of the team will include volunteers, the dying person him- or herself, and the family, all of whom will participate fully in the major decisions regarding management.

For many palliative care workers, their primary task is to address the range of problems presented by dying people and their informal carers. Many of these are summarised in the list of fears below.

- Fear that symptom and pain relief will not be achieved.
- Fear of dying, with the assumption that the process will be painful and unpleasant, or fear of dying alone.
- Fears of alienating others through the illness, for example those who believe the illness is catching or are repulsed by the physical changes in the dying person.
- Fears of death – what is death, what will happen to them when they die, could they be placed in a mortuary or be buried alive?
- Anxieties about those left behind as well as other losses, both in the short term and the long term.

As you proceed through the chapter you will see how these challenges confront the palliative care workers. Sometimes they can be resolved; always they can be acknowledged and shared.

Settings for palliative care

Advances in palliative care have increased the choices available to dying people and the degree to which they can control whatever life is left to them. Sometimes palliative care is not available due to resource constraints. In theory, wherever there is a need for palliative care it should be accessible, as the technical requirements often characterising specialist medical care do not apply. However, not all health providers have access to palliative care services; this particularly applies to the private residential and health care sector, where often the response is to hospitalise the dying person.

There are three settings where palliative care services are likely to be available. Hospice teams vary in composition but tend to employ a comprehensive range of different professionals working in a variety of ways; the co-ordinator is often a palliative care physician. In addition to serving inpatient needs, many hospices have attached home care support teams who care for people dying in the locality. This system has obvious advantages: for example, when someone dying in the community requires medical investigation, or alternatively respite care, the home care team can provide the continuity of care for the dying person as well as his or her family.

Palliative care teams in hospitals usually consist of specialist nurses; occasionally there is a doctor or social worker assigned on a part-time basis. Support and advice are available for hospital staff to help them address the needs of dying people on the wards, as well as for consultation by inpatients and their families. Like hospices, many larger hospitals have home care support teams who provide support to discharged hospital patients.

In many areas it is possible for a dying person to receive palliative care in their own home. The primary care team, led by the general practitioner, sees relatively few dying people per annum; hence the advice of specialists in palliative care can be invaluable, particularly where it is hard to control the dying person's symptoms, or in other complex cases. We have already noted that home care teams work out of local hospices and hospitals; in addition there are teams which are not attached to institutions and are based in a variety of community settings. The structure of home care teams, regardless of their base, varies but will always include specialist nurses, often a part-time doctor, and sometimes a social worker, a counsellor, administrator as well as, often, volunteers. Where no team exists there are often specialist palliative care nurses working out of health centres or independently to provide a service in the community.

Many of these nurses are known as Macmillan nurses because they are financially supported by Cancer Relief Macmillan Fund.

Principles of symptom control

As we have already seen, one of the primary goals of palliative care is to provide symptom relief in order to enable the dying person to enjoy a reasonable quality of life while dying. The overarching principle is to recognise that each dying person is different, with her or his own agenda and needs. The following general principles, adapted from the *Palliative Care Handbook* (Open University, 1993), have been identified in a number of texts describing symptom control.

1 **Accurately diagnose the cause of the symptom**
   It is essential to establish whether the symptom has arisen as a result of the disease or for another reason.

   The cause of symptoms can be multifactorial and so it is necessary to consider each contributory factor. Hence careful history-taking and assessment are required. Consideration of the implications of certain types of treatment may lead to a decision to address the symptom rather than subject the dying person and the carers to intrusive investigations which might in themselves create distress, discomfort and disorientation.

2 **Explain the symptom to the dying person**
   Experiencing some symptoms can be frightening for the dying person and this can in turn exacerbate the symptoms themselves. Professional carers can reassure patients and their relatives by acknowledging the patient's interpretations of the symptoms and then explaining the medical significance of the symptoms.

3 **Discuss alternative treatments**
   To enable dying people to make realistic choices they must be given adequate and interpretable information. The concept of

being consulted about options may be strange for some people, but once curative treatment is no longer an alternative, the person's own ideas of what would be a good quality of life are very relevant. Through participating in decisions about the treatment the dying person will feel in control and valued.

4 **Set attainable goals**
Even when the disease is in an advanced state, dying people will be heartened by the prospect of achieving a particular wish. This could range from being pain-free at night or at rest to being able to swallow or get dressed for a party. Dying people need to be convinced that the carer is competent; if the doctor says the drug will relieve the pain and it does not, the dying person will lose faith in that doctor.

5 **Treat appropriately**
Dying people will rarely understand the origins of pain nor the rationale for certain kinds of treatment. For example, most people assume that intractable pain is caused by disease, not realising that the treatment itself may precipitate pain: for example opiates are renowned for causing constipation, which may be more painful than the cancer.

There is often concern that strong medication might reduce alertness. In addition, dying people may worry about taking 'addictive' drugs. Those prescribing need to be aware of the patient's concerns and try to address them. The responsibility to use medication wisely rests with the prescribing doctor, who runs the risk of the patient's non-compliance if inappropriate medications are recommended.

Both remembering and wanting to take pills on time can be a problem, so minimising the number taken and simplifying instructions will increase the likelihood that the dying person will take the pills. 'Slow release' painkillers reduce the frequency with which pills have to be taken and are available in different strengths so that medication can be changed without the patient having to remember to take more tablets more frequently.

As dying people may require more than one pill four times a day, placing pills in the required square of a 'Dosett Box' simplifies drug-taking for all concerned. Most dying people prefer to take drugs orally, but when this becomes difficult may agree to suppositories; regular injections or intravenous infusions should be avoided where possible. When oral treatment is no longer possible it may be advisable to use a Graseby syringe driver to administer medications – this delivers drugs under the skin through a continuous 24-hour infusion. This mechanism resolves issues regarding timing and operating, because anyone can replenish the drugs as needed. The loan of syringe drivers can usually be arranged through any palliative care worker.

6 **Predict the likely scenarios and plan for them**
Experienced palliative care workers find that they can often forecast which symptoms will develop and hence plan strategically. For example, a very weak dying person may have difficulty swallowing; other ways of giving drugs will need to be found. Prophylactic prescribing of suppositories or injections to ensure continuity of pain relief will reduce the distress experienced by the dying person and the carers. Predicting changes regarding pain control is particularly important when the dying person is at home without ready access to a hospital or hospice pharmacy, or even someone to prescribe alternatives.

7 **Continually inform and support dying people and their relatives**
As we saw in chapter 5, the dying person and all the carers need to be appraised of the developments and supported.

8 **Always present a positive and helpful approach**

Common symptoms in dying people

Most texts on symptom control for dying people focus on the pain experienced by cancer patients, simply because these may be easier to identify and define. However, the principles developed in cancer care can be applied to terminally ill people with a range of conditions. What follows is not a comprehensive list; we have excluded those additional symptoms which also occur in many acutely ill patients, such as incontinence and paralysis. Clearly people confined to bed may develop bedsores, which may be prevented or alleviated by regular turning; this may be painful for the dying person, so another solution such as using special mattresses might be sought.

1 **Weakness**

Most dying people feel debilitated, lethargic and weak, all of which are hard to treat. Weakness is usually caused by progressive disease whereby metabolic changes lead to structural and functional muscle abnormalities. Weakness can be extremely distressing and depressing for dying people as well as their carers, particularly when it results in increased dependency.

Weakness can be addressed in a number of ways, such as providing nutritional support or even appetite stimulants. Treatment, however, may not resolve weakness so it may be best to talk through the problems with the dying person and to encourage positive planning and where possible practical solutions, such as structural changes to living conditions or physiotherapy or hydrotherapy.

2 **Anorexia**

Many people associate the term anorexia with an eating disorder affecting young women, and hence find the term disturbing when used to describe the dying person's loss of appetite and hence apparent unwillingness to eat.

There are a variety of causes of anorexia; these include the locations of disease spread, fear of vomiting, presentation of food (too much), constipation, oral problems such as thrush, biochemical abnormalities, drugs, radiotherapy, depression and anxiety. Food often loses its attractiveness to dying people and the refusal to eat can be frightening for carers who may believe that death will follow by starvation. It is therefore important to understand whose problem it is – the dying person's or the carers'! Carers may need to be reassured that anorexia is simply a feature of the disease and that they are not neglectful if they do not force-feed the dying person – indeed, they are offering that person choice and control. When a dying person recognises that death is inevitable and that food is causing discomfort, that person may be making an informed decision not to eat except when hungry. In addition, in some cultures there are traditions to refrain from food as death approaches, so professional carers should be cautious not to insult the rituals practised by some dying people.

3 Nausea and vomiting

Nausea and vomiting occur in 40% of people with advanced cancer, and many experience these symptoms as very distressing. Nausea and vomiting may have a number of causes such as a response to a drug or radiotherapy, or an additional condition such as hypercalcaemia.

Before embarking on treating nausea and vomiting one should take a careful history to ascertain the cause before deciding whether treatment with anti-emetic (anti-nausea) drugs is appropriate or not. Choosing the appropriate anti-emetics can be problematic as certain preparations exacerbate symptoms and also because each anti-emetic acts on a different site; therefore it may be necessary to use more than one preparation. When the cause is amenable to an anti-emetic it is usually possible to control sensations of nausea and vomiting even in people with advanced disease.

Some people vomit when anxious or have hospital phobia which is manifested by vomiting; this is likely to be best managed by a combination of anti-emetic treatment and counselling or complementary therapies (see below).

4 Constipation

As constipation is a known side-effect of opiates it should be predicted and prophylactically treated. Even though it is one of the most common problems experienced by dying people, carers often dismiss it, assuming that it is an inevitable result of low bulk food intake. Constipation causes a number of other symptoms, such as nausea, abdominal pain, anorexia, lethargy and even confusion.

Laxatives should be prescribed on a regular basis to reduce what may be unnecessary physical as well as emotional distress.

5 **Oedema (water retention)**
Water is often retained in the limbs of dying people, which can make the skin very sore and the limbs swollen. A number of methods may be used to reduce the swellings, for example using special kinds of stockings or bandages. Other ways of reducing swelling may include applying creams or aromatherapy to the affected areas, or encouraging gentle exercise.

6 **Dyspnoea (breathlessness)**
Fifty per cent of people with advanced cancer suffer from dyspnoea, a condition relating to a difficulty in breathing. Dyspnoea is usually caused by the disease, but can be exacerbated by as well as create anxiety. Breathlessness can be frightening for dying people and their carers. In particular, those people with lung disease fear suffocation, and gasping for breath and hence breathlessness can be especially frightening for them.

There are a number of alternative ways of trying to reduce breathlessness. Environmental manipulation would entail ensuring the dying person is cool and in an upright position and not constricted in any way. Sometimes radiotherapy, transfusions or aspirating fluid from the abdomen can reduce dyspnoea. Prescribing nebulised drugs may be experienced as comforting by breathless people. In addition, for those whose breathlessness is anxiety-related, counselling, hypnotherapy or using relaxation tapes may be helpful.

7 **Confusion**
Many dying people experience confusion. The term encompasses many behavioural manifestations but usually suggests a loss of

contact with reality as well as disorientation in time and place. Other symptoms, such as inappropriate behaviour, memory loss, hallucinations, paranoia and incoherent speech, also fall under the umbrella term.

Confusion includes temporary as well as more sustained behavioural changes. It may result from severe constipation or from Alzheimer's Disease; or from secondaries or treatment in people with cancer; and it may fluctuate in cases of arterio-sclerosis.

Confusion can be exacerbated by distress or the responses of other people. Relatives and friends may find seeing the dying person confused distressing or even frightening, particularly if the onset of confusion is sudden. Relatives who are valuing every minute left with their dying relative may find the onset of confusion and consequent lack of meaningful conversation very distressing.

Confusion may not be a permanent state, so in the spirit of palliative care carefully assessing the cause will increase the likelihood of appropriately addressing the problem. In some cases gentle reorientation of the confused person may reconnect that person with reality and enable use of sedation to be avoided. However, should the confused person become agitated or even aggressive and pose a danger to themselves or to others, there may be no alternative but to resort to sedation.

8 **Pain**
Understanding and dealing with pain is an essential component of palliative care. Palliative care strives to understand total pain (see figure 6.1) in order to ascertain, where possible, the origin of the pain, be it physical, psychological or spiritual. Different types of pain interact with one another; for example, psychological distress could be manifested as physical symptoms such as loss of appetite or sleeplessness. Psychological distress might aggravate existing symptoms such as physical pain or nausea, or might also result from the disease.

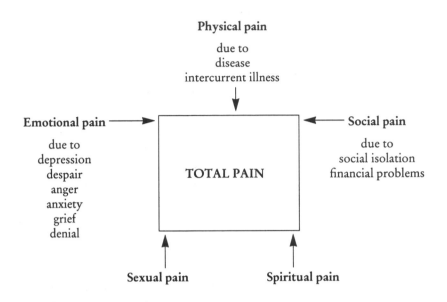

Figure 6.1 Concept of total symptom control
SOURCE: TOOKMAN AND KUROWSKA (1993, P. 6)

Clearly there a number of elements of pain and several ways to address them. First we will look at physical pain in general, then discuss pharmacological treatments, and fears associated by them, followed by complementary therapies.

Physical pain

Many people associate dying with intense physical pain, and hence a terminal diagnosis may fill patients and their carers with trepidation. Tremendous advances have been made in pharmacology and in most cases pain can be alleviated. Palliative specialists emphasise careful assessment of the cause and nature of pain, which usually has a physical basis. Many dying people will have pain at several sites and each should be individually assessed, noting particularly:

- the site of the pain and whether it radiates elsewhere;
- the type and severity of the pain;
- the development and changes in the pain;
- factors which exacerbate or alleviate the pain.

A thorough physical examination should help identify problem spots; it may be necessary to submit the patient to other investigations, but as we have seen these should be avoided wherever possible. It is important to understand the significance of a particular pain or site of pain to the dying person as it may explain the concern or behaviour. For example, a 'minor' unrelated ailment may precipitate considerable distress, but this may underlie other fears and anxieties which need to be sensitively addressed. Also the pain may have implications for mobility or other aspects of the dying person's lifestyle.

Common causes of pain include bone involvement, in cancer, which might be a spread from a variety of primary malignancies in areas such as lung, breast, prostate, kidney and thyroid, or cancer involving the viscera or the nerves. Pain can be caused indirectly by the cancers, as in musculo-skeletal problems, by general debility (see section on 'weakness' above), or by something completely different, such as constipation. It is advisable to distinguish between acute and chronic pain, which may be important when deciding on medication.

To achieve good pain control it is essential regularly to consult the patient, who is best placed to assess its effectiveness; each individual reacts differently to pain and to medication and frequent reassessment is therefore advisable. Dying people and their relatives fear breakthrough pain, and hence it is essential to time the medication carefully. This particularly applies to opiates (see below).

Pain in children

Although this book focuses primarily on dying adults, it is relevant here to note that the problems are different when caring for dying children. Most children who die do so as a result of accidents; those

who die of natural causes suffer from diseases different from
those that affect adults, including congenital disorders and
neurodegenerative conditions. It is important to realise that different
techniques need to be employed to assess a child's pain – what
techniques are used will depend on the child's age, verbal skills and
maturity. Administering drugs will also be more complicated as the
kinds of explanations used with adults will not necessarily work with
children.

Pain relief – pharmacological and surgical

When pain control seems hard to achieve, this may be due to
ineffective use of analgesia or to incorrect assessment of the patient's
pain. Most treatment for pain relief is based on analgesia of differing
strengths, ranging from the lowest level, paracetamol for mild pain,
through mild/moderate pain, where weak opioids can be used, to
moderate/severe pain, where strong opioids such as morphine can be
used. Although opioid analgesia is usually effective, some pain is
only partially sensitive or insensitive to opioid drugs. Hence drugs
other than opioids may contribute to pain relief. These may include
non-steroidal anti-inflammatory drugs, steroids, anti-depressants,
anti-convulsants or anti-spasmodics, depending on the cause of the
pain. With nerve pain, for example, sometimes nerve blockage is
required. This is a surgical intervention usually undertaken by pain
specialists.

Fears about opioids

The term opiate is one with which many people are familiar and
describes naturally occurring compounds derived from the juice of
the opium poppy. Opioid is the term used to describe both naturally
occurring and synthetic narcotic preparations (e.g. diamorphine)
which produce reactions like opiates and morphine. Palliative care
physicians state categorically that 'opioids are safe, effective and
reliable analgesics' (*Palliative Care Handbook*, Open University
1993) and that the most commonly prescribed opioids for dying

people, morphine and diamorphine, should control pain in most patients. If narcotics are prescribed regularly and in adequate doses, and are given early enough and by an appropriate route, the problems occurring should be minimised.

For many dying people, their relatives and even their professional carers, the notion of narcotics and particularly opiates signifies the 'end of the road' as well as the possibility that the patient will become a 'drug addict'. Consequently many dying people do not receive adequate pain relief, as in this description by a staff nurse of the terminal phase of a young person dying of cancer during the mid-1980s:

The next night I came on, Marion had been crossed off her diamorphine and put onto diazepam which did next to nothing for her – I couldn't understand it at all. Anyhow she was very very agitated, she kept trying to get out of bed – you couldn't understand what she was saying and the relatives who were with her were getting very upset and the doctors would not give her any more diamorphine because they said it would have side-effects. So the next day I came on, I said, 'Look, she's got to have something else, she's in a bad way.' The consultant said, no, she did not want to give her diamorphine because she thought she was going to get better, she's in liver failure! The next night I came on, she'd been crossed off her diazepam and all she was on was chlorpromazine; they'd given her a dose of diamorphine at four in the afternoon. I came on and they said, 'She's quite settled now' and I said, 'Well it's not going to last long, is she written up for any more?' No, she wasn't, so I went to the house officer and asked her to write her up for more and she refused because the SHO had written her up for a single dose of diamorphine and he had spoken to the consultant who had said that a single dose of diamorphine was fine but no more. So I said, 'She is going to be all agitated in the night. What am I going to do?' So she said, 'I don't want her to have any more, I've given her the chlorpromazine', but that doesn't do anything.

During the night she started to get very agitated again and the relatives came up to me and said she says she's in pain and I was saying, 'Yes, I know, and there's nothing whatsoever I can do' and I contacted the Nursing Officer and she said, 'If that's what the doctors said then there's nothing you can do.' I got really annoyed and said I'd like to get the consultant up here for her to see what she looks like, and what she is like and what it's doing to her relatives and her boyfriend. It's all right for the consultant, she's in bed, she's not worrying about it, she's not thinking about what this woman is going through.

Marion's boyfriend came into the office and said, 'She's in pain' and he started to get upset and then said, 'I know there's nothing you can do and I shouldn't have said anything' and I said, 'No, you should have done, there is nothing I can do but in the morning will you please talk to the senior house officer and ask him to write her up for some pain relief.' Anyway she died at 7.25 in the morning in terrible pain and I couldn't believe it how they could leave her in such terrible pain. I was really upset that she had to die in so much pain, I knew for three days that she was going to die, so therefore the doctors should have known that and helped her to die peacefully for her sake as well as her relatives.

This case study graphically illustrates the distress that can be experienced by the dying person as well as carers when pain relief is not achieved. In this case the doctors were not present when the dying person was experiencing extreme pain and were unwilling to respond to the requests of their nursing colleagues because of an inherent anxiety about overdosing the patient.

There are several explanations for concern regarding using these drugs, some relating to previous experience when opiates were mixed with other drugs in 'cocktails' producing unwanted side-effects. However, prescribing experience over a number of years has demonstrated that opioids are safe and effective analgesics when measured against pain properly and can be used early on during an illness. Experienced physicians suggest that for those with a limited prognosis, every effort should be made to ensure that whatever life remains should be as pain-free as possible rather than dominated by intractable pain.

Even in professional circles a number of fears still persist about prescribing opioids. The first relates to addiction; this has been dispelled with evidence demonstrating that when opioids are given in the right way for the right conditions they are not addictive. Patients taking opioids for chronic pain do not develop psychological addiction, the condition that scares many people. Physical addiction is likely to occur as it would with many other drugs, in so far as it would be inadvisable suddenly to withdraw a moderate dosage of an opiate from a dying person because of potential unpleasant side-effects. However, one could slowly decrease the dosage with no harmful effects if this were deemed to be best for the patient.

The second fear relates to tolerance; the argument given is that if people are given strong painkillers too soon, there will be nothing left to give them when the pain becomes unbearable. Clinical evidence suggests that this fear is unfounded – most people can remain on a stable dose of morphine for lengthy periods of time and do not become significantly tolerant to oral morphine. The need to increase the dose will relate to increased pain, rather than tolerance. Morphine should not be reserved for the last stages, but started early on rather than using ineffective analgesia. The tendency not to prescribe morphine until the final stages simply reinforces lay perceptions that it should only be used as a last resort.

Some doctors fear that opioids will cause respiratory depression – that breathing will become shallower. If the dose is carefully graduated upwards in relation to the pain experienced, respiratory depression should not be a problem. Others are concerned that morphine may hasten death, not realising that in most cases the quality of life for the dying person is significantly improved through being relatively pain-free.

Thus palliative care emphasises adequate and carefully measured pain relief to minimise discomfort for the dying person whilst maximising quality of life.

Complementary therapies

Many dying people see complementary therapies as a last resort, having found that curative treatments offered by the orthodox establishment have failed. Thus far, trials comparing orthodox and complementary therapies in treating people with cancer have not produced conclusive data, but by the end of the century the scientific trials currently under way should give some indication of the relative effectiveness of different therapies.

However, complementary therapies may improve the quality of life for dying people and their families. A word of caution is nonetheless in order. Some of the therapies, particularly those which focus exclusively on diet, may exacerbate physical damage; others may offer false hope of cure and hence lead to great disappointment and disillusionment. At the same time, many therapies work well alongside conventional medicine, alleviating emotional as well as physical distress.

Several complementary therapists are integrated into some hospice and palliative care teams to address the full range of 'total pain'. There is a wide range of therapists working in this field, practising therapies including osteopathy, aromatherapy, herbalism, spiritual healing, meditation, massage, visualisation, homeopathy, hypnotherapy, reflexology and acupuncture. In addition, counselling, medical visualisation and spiritual healing are directed at the dying person's psyche. The case study of Mrs Winter shows how one complementary therapy was used.

MRS WINTER

Mrs Winter had suffered several strokes by the time she was 60 and eventually her husband could not manage to nurse her alone at home. She was admitted to the geriatric ward of the local district general hospital where her state deteriorated rapidly. Her concentration diminished and following several further strokes she became mentally incapacitated. She no longer recognised her family but seemed to relax and seem less agitated during their visits. Mrs Winter appeared to be attached to a particular nurse and when this nurse left the ward she became constantly agitated, crying out and being seen as a 'disturbance'.

A family friend suggested to Mr Winter that she had seen a television programme about aromatherapy, where older stroke patients responded well to the massage and the aromas of the oils. Mr Winter asked the charge nurse if he knew of a local aromatherapist because he wondered whether this would help his wife. The charge nurse had never heard of aromatherapy but agreed to investigate the possibilities. After many requests to hospital authorities, who were most sceptical, an aromatherapist was found to visit Mrs Winter, and try to calm her using oils and massage. The hospital was unable to find funds to pay the aromatherapist but Mr Winter's children agreed to pay for this service as they hoped it might relieve Mrs Winter's anxiety. The first few sessions were difficult for both parties – Mrs Winter seemed to stiffen up and become more agitated; however, the aromatherapist felt that once she found the appropriate scent Mrs Winter would respond positively to the scent as well as the massage. After five sessions, Mrs Winter was much calmer, and it was decided to maintain this therapy indefinitely.

As yet, trained practitioners in complementary medicine are not widely available and cost structures vary. Some hospices and palliative care teams have contact with several complementary practitioners and report that dying people treated by them derive considerable comfort and a sense of well-being from these therapies.

The 'comfort' factor can be seen as the interface between pain resulting from organic causes and that resulting from non-physical causes. The next chapter will begin by continuing to explore the 'pain' experienced by dying people, but will focus on their emotional, psychological and spiritual concerns as death approaches. These may be present throughout a terminal illness but may become more acute when death is imminent and will require to be dealt with in a sensitive manner for the sake of all concerned.

7

As death approaches

This chapter will focus on events just prior to and immediately following death. As this period can be difficult for everyone we will start by exploring how to discover and then address the needs and wishes of dying people and their carers when death nears. Where the person dies will somewhat determine the range of possible responses, so we will examine the restraints imposed by different settings. The second half of the chapter will describe in detail practical procedures required after someone has died; these include laying out the body and registering the death. This 'practical' informative section will help you to smoothe the way for bereaved relatives and friends to carry out these procedures.

Quality of life as death approaches

In previous chapters we looked at some of the problems and possibilities of addressing the wishes of dying people and their carers. However, the whole concept of enabling people to express their needs as they approach the terminal stages is problematic. Asking a dying person what he or she wants will not ensure that that person will feel comfortable or confident enough to verbalise or otherwise indicate their wishes. Each person is subject to personal pressures, be they their own inhibitions or views, or cultural or social restraints. Through demonstrating that one is not judgemental and is genuinely empathetic, it may be possible to get to know the dying person and their relatives. This is not an easy task; it requires time and patience and may be complicated by the dying person's changing moods or the relatives making what appear to be unreasonable demands. Sensitive awareness to a fluid and possibly volatile situation may improve chances of achieving good communication. Confronting many different issues at the same time as providing meals and drugs on time is difficult and sometimes impossible because of logistical constraints. Carers may experience considerable frustration trying to expedite some wish and being unsuccessful.

For many people dying in an unfamiliar place, over which they have little or no control, means that their own particular customs or habits are compromised. Understanding all the foibles and all the needs of individual dying people is an impossible task, but ascertaining certain habits which provide the security of a routine for that dying person may help make their dying a better experience.

Carers will thus want to address the whole range of needs of the dying person as death nears, including spiritual, emotional, physical and practical needs. The major challenge is how to establish those needs and address them in a sensitive, efficient and yet unrushed manner. A goal will be to maintain as far as possible the autonomy of the dying person, when mental faculties are waning or the dying person appears to be aware but is unable to express wishes verbally. Keeping the dying person central may be difficult for a variety of reasons – relatives may intervene or a particular wish may be impossible to grant.

Addressing practical problems

Some practical issues relate to personal preferences and practices that may arise as death approaches. Frances Sheldon (1993), a social worker who lectures in palliative care, talks about the problems of prioritising when we have limited resources available: How can one differentiate between someone's needs and their wants? With, for example, only one single room available, how do we make the decision to allocate that room? Many dying people will want to carry on 'normal living' while dying yet are prevented by institutional barriers from doing what they would normally do in other settings. As death approaches, some people will want to be alone and not disturbed. Is providing a single room for someone who is dying meeting a need or a want? If you're having to make a choice, in other words, depriving one person from the privacy they desire while granting the same facility to someone else, what criteria should you use? Frances Sheldon suggests that placing someone who may be disruptive or confused in a single room might be perceived as a need, but wouldn't an older single woman who has never shared a room before also be justified in having a single room – or a young husband who wants privacy to be with his wife? These problems are difficult to address.

Logistically it may be straightforward to fulfil the wish of someone who wants a nurse to be available or a friend to sit quietly and provide reassurance. But sometimes enabling the dying person to have many people around may pose difficulties. Jews, Muslims, Hindus, Sikhs and Christians may want to observe their religious rituals and have members of their faith saying prayers for or with them. Racism exists in Britain; how can dying people and their relatives be protected from hurtful comments or demeaning postures by health workers as well as by other patients and their relatives?

As death nears issues often arise relating to pain control and other medication. The need to provide sufficient pain control was illustrated by the case study of Marion in the previous chapter (page 109). This demonstrated the links between effective pain relief and good communication between carers. You will recall how in Marion's case inadequate pain relief affected not only the dying woman but her relatives, friends and the nurses caring for her. She was agitated and trying to get out of bed. For her, being in physical pain exacerbated her emotional distress – everyone knew she was dying but no one could calm her or have a meaningful leavetaking because of her physical discomfort.

Withdrawing medications may be interpreted by the dying person as a sign that all hope for recovery is lost and cause distress. As in the case study of Marion, medical staff may insist that additional medication could be 'harmful'. Alternatively, the dying person may want treatment stopped, or refuse to eat, which may create conflicts for carers. Does the dying person want additional medication and to what extent? Is the dying person comfortable or should the position be changed? It may be hard to maintain a balance, appearing confident and competent without being intrusive, as well as getting answers to these questions sufficiently quickly to ensure the dying person's wishes are met.

Emotional distress

In chapter 2 we discussed what Elisabeth Kubler-Ross terms 'acceptance' – the final stage of emotional preparation for dying. There are some dying people who refuse to accept the finality of death and fight it all the way. This can be uncomfortable for carers, who may wish to delve and find out that person's concerns and fears and provide some support. On the other hand, those accepting the reality may want the opportunity to talk and explore their feelings with friends, relatives or professionals. However, actually verbalising fears and anxieties to friends, relatives and professionals may be difficult for the dying person for many many reasons. Saying, 'I'm frightened and sad because I'm dying' may evoke an intolerable response and the dying person may no longer have the capability or strength to cope with the emotions this evokes. Many dying people will want to keep their thoughts to themselves and so helping them through counselling or medication or complementary therapies may not be helpful. Settings as well as personality characteristics impose constraints on the possibilities available to informal as well as professional carers when they try to allay the anxieties of someone nearing death.

Emotional distress may be experienced as physical pain as well as being aggravated by inadequate medical treatment. Many dying people will be anxious regardless of their physical state. Distress could be manifested by behaviour such as being unusually aggressive or appearing to withdraw and to be very tired. Drug treatments, although not a substitute for other interventions may be appropriate to improve the dying person's quality of life whether for physical or psychological pain.

Language and cultural differences may also contribute to emotional distress. Health workers may encounter Muslims, for example, from different countries speaking a number of languages, who are unfamiliar or uncomfortable with the norms of British social relationships. This applies particularly to the older age group and women. Modesty is central to South Asian people, whether Muslims or Hindus, and Asian women may not want to be examined or touched by male health workers, although sometimes they will agree if another woman is present. Some Muslim men will apply this in reverse, not wanting to be touched by female health workers.

Another cultural difference which might make a dying person anxious relates to observing religious dietary laws. In some instances that person will not want to eat institutional food or accept plates used by other patients, and may feel constrained from expressing this wish. Ritual washing is also customary in some religions, and requesting a basin may evoke a negative response which might hurt the dying person. This is an important cultural tradition and Hindus and Sikhs will require water for ritual cleansing before and after prayer and for washing after excreting and urinating; Sikhs will also wish to rinse out their mouths before eating and before prayer; observant Jews will want to wash before eating bread.

Spiritual needs

In chapter 6 we identified spiritual needs as a central element of palliative care. But this is a hard subject to deal with. Frances Sheldon (1993) separates out some of the issues: 'Who should discuss it with patients, how should they do so, how we recognise when patients are talking about it and how we ensure that no pressure is put on patients to take up a particular spiritual stance – these issues have not been fully resolved.' You will recall from the case study in chapter 2 (page 25) the distress displayed by Ramjit's family that he died alone, and the implications of this for their future lives as well as their concern for his soul. Those without a formal religion may also agonise over life and death issues, or try to puzzle out what may seem to be unfair, asking 'why me?' questions. Many people have a concept of what they see as a good death – in Marion's case, the family saw it as a pain-free, anxiety-free experience. Hindus like to prepare for what they see as a good death, which would be accompanied by the minimum of excretions – hence they will want to fast in preparation. For Hindus in particular (although the same applies to many relatives from a wide range of backgrounds), the dying person's last words or actions affect the experience of bereavement; some religions believe that unless particular practices are performed at the dying moment and after death, the soul's route will be impeded. Hence the actions and attitudes of professional carers can have considerable significance to dying people and their relatives.

As immigrant populations age and British health workers confront religious and cultural death rituals more frequently, education regarding the range of practices and rituals surrounding death becomes more urgent. For religious groupings that are dislocated from their origins and extended families, the death of their relatives in a society antipathetic to their practices is likely to be traumatic. They require sensitive responses to feel enabled to practise their rituals without shame or embarrassment.

Despite emphasis on racial awareness in many settings, unfamiliar customs that disrupt routines still unsettle health workers. Increased education for health workers is necessary to familiarise them with the common rituals. By acknowledging ignorance of customs and asking the dying person or his or her relatives appropriate questions, health workers may enable individuals and families to observe particular rituals in the ways they would wish to. Through understanding the impact their behaviour may have on the bereaved, health workers may develop the sensitivity and skills needed to guide and protect bereaved people who are members of ethnic minorities.

It is important to emphasise again that dying is an intensely personal affair and that stereotyped assumptions about practices to be observed based on race or creed should not be made. Many people in Britain are affiliated at some level to the Christian faith, within which there is a large variation of rituals pertaining to death. In addition, those nominally affiliated to one branch of Christianity may not observe as many practices as those who see themselves as practising Christians – hence for one Roman Catholic the presence of a priest administering last rites will be a crucial step to the next world, for another the presence of a priest may be distressing. In addition to the variation of religious rituals there are family traditions that people want to observe. Essentially, everyone should be given the same respect and asked the same questions. However, health workers trying to facilitate the carrying out of people's wishes may find themselves constrained by a number of obstacles imposed by, for example, the nature of the setting.

Settings and barriers

Each location imposes its own barriers and restraints, and limits the choices available to the dying person and informal carers. However hard one tries, there are inevitably real barriers to facilitating a good death in an institution. Routines, structures, pressure of work, demands from other patients and from superiors all conspire to prevent carers from providing an individualised service to a dying person. It is difficult to create a homely atmosphere in a busy acute ward or an outpatient department. It is less difficult to convey an unrushed atmosphere in a hospice ward. Hence it is important to remember that the context in which death occurs determines to a large extent the way in which it is experienced by all concerned.

In chapter 2 we explored the range of choices of the place of death and some factors that influence that choice. The dying process will vary from person to person and all the carers will want to ensure that the physical and emotional needs of the dying person are met, as well as to be reassured themselves.

Routines for dealing with dying people in institutional settings often seem to exist primarily for the benefit of those staffing the institution. These routines may prevent the inclusion of others who want to be involved in the last moments of the dying person. These may be other residents in homes for older people, or relatives and friends in other institutions. Very often, a death in an overstretched NHS hospital provides a bed for another acutely ill person; hence staff are encouraged to perform last offices as quickly as possible and take the body off the ward. This may conflict with staff perceptions of their own needs and the need of the relatives to sit with the body for a while and lay out the body when it feels right.

Caring for relatives

Notifying relatives and friends that death has occurred can be a traumatic task for health workers. In the next chapter we discuss at some length the difficulties inherent in this task after accidental death, but what if the death is to some degree anticipated? Who should call the relatives? Should this information be broken over the phone, or should relatives be told that the 'situation is grave' and they should come at once? Breaking bad news, as we saw in chapter 4, is always difficult and pitching it at the right level with an appropriate empathetic approach is not easy.

Once the relatives have arrived at the institution, be it a hospital, hospice or residential home, how should they be treated? Some institutions prefer that relatives are first taken into an office and given a cup of tea before seeing the body. This procedure may depend on the religious practices of the relatives or the deceased, and we shall deal with this in detail below. Certain relatives or friends may find it particularly difficult to request access to the body because the relationship that they had with the deceased was secret or private. This applies particularly to gay partners and partners in extramarital liaisons.

Dying at home, while providing comfort and familiarity for the dying person, may be frightening and create confusion for others. As death nears, there can be pressure from relatives, friends or even the GP to hospitalise the dying person, usually relating to a belief that the pain may not be manageable at home.

When a death is anticipated and discussed in advance, and a decision taken to keep the dying person at home, those present will be prepared for the necessary procedures after death has occurred – calling the GP to certify the death before calling a funeral director or making other arrangements for disposing of the body. When the death is sudden and unexpected, with a sudden collapse either in the house or in the street, the normal response is to call for an ambulance. Sometimes when ambulance staff arrive they inform those present that the person is already dead and advise calling a GP to certify death rather than taking the body to hospital. This situation can be frightening and confusing for those left with the body, and they will require sensitive advice as well as practical help. The dramatic change of appearance of someone after death can be quite shocking for those present, even those working with acutely ill patients. The following quote from a nurse illustrates this:

> *I was really shocked when I saw Mrs Grace, it didn't seem true for a while, she changed so much, I couldn't believe that she was so different – she was so bubbly, happy and jolly and to see her lying there she was all grey and oh it was eerie, just lying there she was nothing, you know, one minute she was something alive and we were all caring for her and the next minute she was sort of gone ...*

If some nurses respond in this way, it is understandable that relatives finding themselves alone with a body can be frightened and confused.

Laying out

Unless there are reasons to the contrary, last offices will be performed shortly after death whatever the setting. Reasons for avoiding laying out include religious prohibitions as well as legal restrictions. Before laying out a Jewish, Muslim, Hindu or Sikh body, permission should be sought from the family as these religions specify ritual cleansing to be undertaken by people who are specially trained.

Deaths must be reported to a coroner in a variety of cases. If someone has died following surgery or another procedure or within a day of admission to hospital, or if the cause of death is unknown or suspected to be of unnatural causes, the death must be reported to a coroner. In such events the deceased should be left as he or she is, with no tubes or drains moved, to facilitate a post mortem.

Laying out entails cleaning and tidying the body, in short making it presentable for others to see as well as maintaining modesty and privacy for the deceased. In most UK health care institutions nurses lay out the body. Relatives are rarely included, but some might welcome an invitation to do so. The wishes of relatives should be taken into account, again taking particular care to ensure that religious rituals can be observed.

When someone dies at home, laying out may be done by district nurses or alternatively by funeral directors, usually at their own premises. It is important to lay the deceased out before rigor mortis makes this difficult – about three hours after death.

The procedure

The following outline of the laying-out procedure is adapted from Green and Green (1992).

Blankets should be removed and the body covered with a sheet; the head should be supported by a small pillow. Keeping the body flat is important to ensure that it will fit on a trolley as well as in the coffin. All clothing should be removed and the body checked for any unexpected marks, which should be reported to the doctor before proceeding. The eyes should be closed, even if this requires using an adhesive. The mouth, which may be open, should be cleaned thoroughly before being gently bandaged closed until the body has stiffened, when the bandages can be removed. Tight bandaging can leave marks and should be avoided.

The bladder should be emptied and the bowels and vagina packed with cotton wool to avoid any serious leakage (incontinence pads can be used to soak up subsequent spillage). It is important to stem as much as possible leakage of any bodily fluids because of potential danger of infection to those caring for the deceased. Any other potential sources of leakage, such as sites where needles or drainage tubes were attached or unhealed surgical incisions, will also need to be securely covered with waterproof tape. Clips and stitches should not be changed.

The body is cleaned thoroughly in the following order: first the front, including the face, ears and nose; then the back, ensuring that sores are covered with waterproof dressings. An incontinence pad should be placed under the deceased and the undersheet, if soiled, replaced. Men without beards should be shaved; hair and nails should be clean and neat. Any jewellery left on the body should be recorded on the card accompanying the body, noting as many descriptive details as possible. In most cases jewellery should be removed and labelled in the presence of witnesses. Where the deceased is a Sikh the symbols of their faith (the 5Ks) should not be disturbed – these are uncut hair, a wooden comb holding the hair, a metal bracelet on the right wrist, the symbolic sword in a sheath and the short trousers (or underwear). A male Sikh's hair is always covered by a turban, even in death, having been sanctified at initiation into the faith.

Identification of the body is essential. In hospitals ankle bracelets are usually used. Mortuary staff and funeral directors often write a number to identify the corpse on the foot or leg. The body is covered with a shroud made of plastic or paper and then wrapped in a sheet to keep it straight. It is then ready for the mortuary.

When death takes place at home, the funeral directors will often lay out the body in their own premises and will collect the body from the house. Sometimes they place the body in a body bag which can be distressing for relatives who may prefer the use of a stretcher. This may in practice be impossible, and using a body bag unavoidable. In addition, with increased awareness of health risks to 'death workers' the preference for using body bags is understandable; even so, sensitivity for relatives' feelings should be shown by those taking away the deceased.

Feelings about laying out

Touching a corpse is often feared for many reasons, one of which may be 'contagion'. Superstitions about corpses may discourage some informal carers from participating in laying out. For nurses, laying out is part of their job, but many find it 'morbid', distressing or frightening. The quotes below reflect some of the range of opinion regarding laying out among the nurses we studied on the cancer ward:

> *Agnes died early one morning and we'd just come on duty and her body was still on the ward and one of the staff nurses couldn't lay her out because she'd become quite attached to her, she was quite upset and had known her longer than perhaps any of us and she couldn't do the last offices.*

> *When laying out I feel very quiet – some nurses think 'fine, they're dead, that's it' and don't show any respect and just treat it as a lump of meat. I get very upset about that, I don't like to see their bodies exposed and I don't like to see them lying on the bed naked because I always think there's something around [a spirit] and if that was me I wouldn't like someone treating me like that – the one thing I hate more than anything is wrapping them up in a sheet and tying it over their face because I think they won't be able to breathe, you know, suffocate, I don't know why.*

> *The first time we laid anyone out between us we sort of detached ourselves from the situation by going through the procedure by saying, 'this is point one, this is point two, point three' and again we weren't emotionally involved in it.*

Thus some nurses found laying out stressful, particularly if they knew the deceased well; to cope with this they would divorce themselves from the personality of the 'body', or if they did not know the deceased would perform the laying out in a mechanistic way. However, for most of the nurses studied laying out presented an opportunity to talk to the body and express initial grief. Many nurses wanted to lay out patients they had tended, seeing it as their ultimate duty to the patient and felt it enabled them to express their grief and work through their own feelings. When laying out was not permitted for religious or legal reasons they felt cheated and distressed at not being able to prepare the deceased for 'their last journey' as the following case study reflects:

MICHAEL

Michael was the 'star' patient of Everett ward. He was nineteen and had been the ward mascot for eight years. Michael had been a 'success story' initially, having gone into remission for his malignancy for several years. Even during the past three years since his relapse he retained his special place and was chosen to be interviewed for a television programme about the work on the ward. The ward staff were very involved with Michael, proud of his A level results and his university achievements. His mother was also integrated into the nursing culture on the ward.

Michael's family were observant Jews. Rabbis were frequent visitors to the ward and knew the nurses. However, when Michael's condition started to deteriorate and he went into a coma, the nurses sensed that they were not very welcome in Michael's room. The rabbis asked that they did not move him and promised to take good care of him. The family made it clear that it was Jewish practice to keep the dying person company, keep their spirits up and recite psalms and other prayers with them but refrain from touching them. When Michael died, the student nurses wanted to spend some time alone with him, talk to him about their good times together and lay him out in the normal fashion. They saw this as their last opportunity to do something for Michael with whom they identified.

However, it was explained to the nurses that Michael would not be laid out in the usual way. First of all, according to Jewish law Michael could not be moved till death had been confirmed. Then they were told to handle the body as little as possible, close his eyes and mouth, remove all tubes, straighten the body, cover him with a white sheet and angle the bed so that his feet faced the door. The rabbis told the nurses that they would keep watch over Michael in the customary way until he was collected by the Chevra Kaddisha (Jewish Burial Society) who would take him to their own premises, where trained members of the same sex as the deceased would ritually cleanse (tahara) and dress Michael's body and place him in the coffin ready for burial as soon as this could be arranged.

Although the nurses respected Michael's faith and had learned much about Judaism from him, they found that being deprived of carrying out 'last offices' left them feeling as if they had not completed their nursing tasks properly.

Health workers may not be aware of religious beliefs or practices associated with death. Judaism, Islam, Hinduism and Sikhism, for example, each specify rites for the dying person as well as the procedures to deal with the body. In all these religions the body of the deceased must be protected, while the soul is seen as sacrosanct. The concept of protecting the body was echoed by the nurses we studied. They were incensed when porters collecting corpses handled them roughly and ensured that the journey to the mortuary was conducted in a dignified manner.

Registration of deaths

After someone has died it is necessary to obtain medical certification of death. In institutions this is usually arranged by staff members. Hospitals and hospices will normally have a resident doctor to certify death, whereas in a residential home certification may take longer. Administrators will be available to explain the required procedures to bereaved relatives.

The legal requirements can be very confusing and distressing to mourners. If the death was unexpected, several people need to be notified – the general practitioner, the next of kin, the deceased's minister of religion (if relevant) and the police, who will help in locating next of kin if necessary. If the death may not be due to natural causes, the body should not be touched and the coroner should be notified.

It is important to ascertain whether the deceased had a will and, if so, whether they had specified burial or cremation. Some people belong to burial schemes or donate their bodies to science. For transplant purposes the latter is of extreme urgency as most organs must be removed within 30 minutes of death.

If the cause of death is apparent the certifying doctor will give the relatives a medical certificate (specifying this) and a formal notice which explains how the death should be registered. The doctor will report the death to the coroner if it was caused by an accident or injury or industrial disease or occurred during a surgical procedure, or if the cause is unknown, sudden and unexplained. In addition, a death must be reported to a coroner if the deceased had not been seen by a doctor during the fatal illness.

Sometimes an autopsy (also known as a post-mortem) is required by law or requested by the hospital. This is a detailed investigative procedure undertaken in the autopsy suite of a mortuary to attempt to ascertain the cause of death. Where autopsies are requested by the hospital this can be for research and educational purposes or a way of auditing staff performance. Post mortems advance medical science by helping to explain disease processes or the effects of treatment. Under these circumstances relatives can demand an explanation for the autopsy, request that organs are returned to the body or even refuse to grant permission.

Coroners' post mortems, which examine 'unnatural causes of death', take place either in a hospital or in a local authority mortuary. 'Unnatural causes' include suicide, murder and road accidents. Permission from relatives is not required as coroners' post mortems fulfil a legal requirement. Post mortems are forbidden by Judaism and Islam and disliked by Hindus, but may nonetheless be insisted upon by the coroner. Where autopsies are performed on Jews and Muslims, the organs should be returned to the body for burial. Explaining to relatives the reasons for the autopsy may reduce some of the distress experienced. Holding up the release of bodies by legal authorities can create tremendous distress for Jews and Muslims (who bury their dead) and Hindus and Sikhs (who cremate their dead), because all these religions specify rapid disposal for the sake of the deceased as well as the bereaved.

An inquest is held if the post mortem reveals that death was not from natural causes, or if death was a result of medical negligence. The inquest will try to ascertain when the person died, how, where and for what reason. It does not apportion blame. Sometimes a jury is appointed to reach a verdict. The rules in Scotland differ from those in England; north of the border a procurator-fiscal handles death from 'unnatural causes'.

Certification of death varies among the countries of the United Kingdom, and moving the body from one to another may create some paperwork. Department of Health and Department of Social Security pamphlets provide up-to-date information for each country and should be available to charge nurses, heads of homes and bereaved people. There are special forms for certifying stillbirths which register both the birth and the death of the baby. These also have to be obtained before removing the body for disposal. The number of forms and procedures can be confusing and complicated for grieving friends and relatives, and efforts should be concentrated on facilitating a smooth process from death to disposal.

Once the legal requirements have been attended to, bereaved people can proceed with making arrangements to bury or cremate the body. Contacting funeral directors and notifying relatives and colleagues that someone has died is for many people a stressful process. The next two chapters will explore how bereaved people experience grief and mourning.

8

The immediate impact of bereavement

In chapter 1 we discussed some patterns of reactions to loss, whether it is the prospect of losing one's own life or that of a loved one. Profound shock, often accompanied with a difficulty in comprehending the impact of the loss, is a common immediate reaction to bereavement. This, of course, will depend on many factors: the closeness of the bond to the dead person, the degree of dependency, the age of the dead person and the relationship to the bereaved are all important. But shock and disbelief are likely to be more acute when the death is sudden and unexpected. The events surrounding the death and the manner in which the news of the death is conveyed to the bereaved person can have a lasting effect for good or ill. People say they remember with the utmost clarity the words and gestures with which the news of the death of a loved one is conveyed. People in a professional capacity have the opportunity and responsibility to mitigate the worst of that shock by taking care that they convey the news as sensitively as possible and provide the initial support that may be needed. Breaking bad news has been dealt with extensively in chapter 4 and much of that discussion is relevant to breaking the news of the death to the person bereaved. In this chapter we will look at how the impact of both sudden and unexpected deaths and anticipated deaths can be mitigated in the period immediately following the death. We will also consider the special difficulties that parents face when they lose a child, at whatever age, including the situations of stillbirths, neonatal deaths and cot deaths.

Sudden and unexpected deaths

Deaths which occur without warning, due to accidents or injury or other causes, frequently take place in the casualty (A&E) departments of hospitals. These can be frightening places; they are designed for efficiency and clinical need and are not places of comfort and calm. Yet it is in this atmosphere that many people experience the death of a loved one. If they were not aware of the accident then they will have received the news from police personnel and arrive at casualty in a highly charged state. How can casualty departments provide a supportive setting for people who are bereaved, and how can busy casualty staff provide for their needs as well as attending to the other demands on their attention? The following account documents how one casualty department has acknowledged and dealt with this problem. As you read it make a mental note of its important features.

SUPPORT IN THE ACCIDENT AND EMERGENCY DEPARTMENT

On arrival in the department, friends and relatives of critically ill or injured patients are taken to a specially furnished relatives' room by a nurse, who stays with them and provides an honest interpretation of the patient's progress. All staff are taught the importance of continuous support and communication with non-technical language. The relatives' room is adjacent to the resuscitation area but opens on to a quiet corridor with toilets nearby. It contains sofas and easy chairs, facilities for making tea, a mirror, a box of tissues and a direct dial telephone. Carpets, wallpaper, curtains and a table lamp create a warm, domestic environment. Some relatives ask to witness the resuscitation, and this is encouraged after explanation by the nurse. Frequent reports of developments are essential. News of deterioration or death is given by the most senior members of staff managing the patient. Repeated, simple explanations and listening and sharing are important. Spiritual support is immediately available, but a priest is not approached without the relatives agreeing.

If the patient dies the body is moved into a private room. Relatives and friends, including children, are encouraged to visit and stay in the room as long as they wish. If the patient was a child or baby the relatives are encouraged to hold the body. Subsequent communication with the coroner's officer, general practitioner, health visitor, social services and clergy follows standard practice.

When the patient's relatives and friends have left, the medical and nursing staff are given support. They are encouraged to take a few minutes for quiet discussion and to share feelings, and this time is considered invaluable.

(*Source*: Yates, Ellison and McGuiness, 1993, pp. 280–1)

Having a separate room away from the hectic atmosphere of the casualty department seems essential for privacy and dignity if situations where relatives are left to fend for themselves in the general mêlée of the casualty department are to be avoided. Making the space as homely as possible should help prevent the fear that A&E departments can generate. But perhaps the most important aspect of this account is the way the staff communicate and relate to relatives and friends. Trouble is taken to explain what is happening and to keep them informed of developments; and they are allowed to witness the resuscitation if they feel they want to. This can be particularly important if the person has not been formally identified, and the sooner this can be effected the better to avoid the agonising suspense of uncertainty. After a death they are encouraged to stay with the body for as long as they wish and to touch and hold the dead person. Relatives often value help and support when approaching the dead body of someone they love; it can be frightening and they often don't know what is expected of them. They may feel inhibited in touching the body in the alien surroundings of a hospital. But time spent with the body after a sudden bereavement can help to dispel feelings of disbelief and help people to accept the reality of the situation. It helps if the body is presented in as decent a state as possible; if the body is mutilated then the relatives will need to be prepared for this. Religion may dictate who may and may not touch the body and staff should be aware of the different customs. Muslims, Hindus, Sikhs and Jewish

l only by a member of the same sex from

for

—— —. —are for bereaved people is not easy or cheap. But if staff are to give the sensitive support that suddenly bereaved people are likely to need there are resource implications. In this particular department all the medical and nursing staff had received training in the initial support of suddenly bereaved people from a special bereavement counsellor who worked in the department and whose role included counselling, teaching and actual nursing. It is also acknowledged that staff too are affected by a death and support is available for them.

The death of a child

Sudden and unexpected bereavement is usually very difficult to deal with. When the death involves a child then it is perhaps even more distressing. The Society of Compassionate Friends, a self-help nationwide organisation which aims to help bereaved parents, claims that 'there is no death so sad' as the death of a child. Thankfully, death in childhood is not common. But that in itself has implications for those whose child does die. There are few people with whom to share the experience, and it is something every parent dreads. People in both their professional and private lives may therefore find it hard to give comfort and support to those who do experience such an event. Approximately 10,000 children die each year. Well over half of these deaths are due to accidents, either on the roads or at home. The other half are due to life-threatening diseases. There are also about 2,000 babies who die each year in the United Kingdom, of which about 1,500 are diagnosed as cases of Sudden Infant Death Syndrome or 'cot death'.

Cot deaths

The immediate impact of these deaths is devastating and in the case of Sudden Infant Death Syndrome the lack of a known cause creates especially distressing conditions around the death of the baby. As you read through the following account of a 'cot death' note the particular features which are likely to add to the distress of losing one's baby and think how these might be mitigated.

———— THE DEATH OF PETER ————

Peter was ten weeks old when he died. His mother and father, Julie and Steven, were quite young – both in their early twenties – and Peter was their first child. Julie and Steven had lived together for about two years, and although they were not married and the pregnancy was not planned they were both very happy to be parents. Steven was a psychiatric nurse and Julie worked in a bank, so they both had fairly secure jobs. Peter was much loved. Julie was just coming to the end of her allocated maternity leave and was a little worried about leaving the baby, but her mother had promised to help and as Steven worked shifts they were hoping to manage without incurring the costs of a childminder. Julie was just beginning to feel confident about being a mother, having been very nervous at first. She had persevered with breast-feeding although she had not found it easy, but now was into a routine which would have to be altered when she went back to work.

Julie and Steven only had a small flat and were hoping to move into something larger quite soon. Since his birth Peter had slept in his cot in their bedroom which they hadn't minded because it saved using any elaborate baby alarm systems. It was therefore a terrible shock for Steven to find Peter lifeless in his cot when he looked at him before going on to early shift. Julie woke to see Steven desperately trying to breathe life into Peter, but with no effect. Neither of them could believe that they had put him to bed a well and contented child and that he had somehow died in the night while they slept beside him. They wrapped him in a blanket and drove him straight to the casualty department in the vain hope that there was some way of bringing him back to life.

The casualty officer was very kind and gently told them that Peter was indeed dead and probably had been dead for about three hours. Because there was no obvious cause he told them that a post mortem would have to be carried out and he hinted at 'other' procedures. Peter was taken away and a nurse took Steven and Julie into sister's office and gave them a cup of tea which they held on to for comfort. Unfortunately it was the time for the change of shift, and so they were moved out as the day staff came bustling in. They sat in the waiting area, not knowing what they were waiting for. When the handover of staff was complete, Steven went to ask the day sister what was happening. She said they could go home as soon as the police had been to take a statement. They were dumbfounded and their nightmare took on other proportions. Neither in their shock had thought to contact either of their own parents and so Steven asked sister if he could use a telephone. Conveying such news to the grandparents was too much for Steven and he broke down. Sister allowed them both to stay in her office while they waited for the police. As they waited Julie began to feel a strange dampness on the front of her tee-shirt and realised with horror that it was well past the time for Peter's early morning feed and her milk was overflowing. Fortunately Julie's parents arrived and Julie collapsed like a child herself into her mother's arms. Everything seemed to happen at once. The police came to take the statement; Julie was not capable of dealing with this and Steven told them everything he knew. Then Steven had to go with the police to identify the body of his son in the hospital mortuary. He was glad that Julie had not come with him as it was a cold and bleak place. Steven wanted to take Peter home with them but was told that he had not yet had his post mortem examination and that they would be able to take him from the undertakers as soon as it was completed. It would probably be later that day. There was nothing else to do but go home and wait. Julie's mother felt that Julie needed help and asked the GP to call. It was the first she had heard about it and was very sympathetic. She gave Julie some advice about suppressing her lactation and also left a prescription for sleeping tablets as she warned them that it would be difficult to sleep at night in the same room in which Peter had died. Later that day Steven and his father went to the undertaker's with the intention of bringing Peter back home. When they saw Peter they hardly recognised him due to the necropsy and they decided that it would be best if he was to remain in the undertaker's chapel of rest. Julie insisted on going to see him but afterwards regretted it because he no longer resembled her child. Only then did it hit her that in all the confusion she had not held him and said goodbye before he had been subjected to this mutilation. That has remained a source of deep regret for both Steven and Julie.

In this case, unlike the casualty department described earlier, there was no quiet room where bereaved relatives could be private. The staff tried to give the parents comfort but it was not easy at such a busy time of the morning with the handover of staff. Had they known how events would unfold, Julie and Steven might not have been in such a hurry to take Peter to the hospital and on reflection wished they had called in their GP and waited at home. It would have been helpful if the casualty officer, who knew what the procedures were, had given them the opportunity to hold Peter and to make their farewells before he was taken to the mortuary.

The GP had been helpful in recognising the distress that continuing lactation would cause and in advising them that they might need the help of sleeping tablets. The fact that Peter died while they slept is likely to make sleep difficult for them for some time.

Unfortunately, in spite of research and the work of the Foundation for Sudden Infant Death Syndrome (FSIDS), 'cot deaths' are still surrounded in mystery and so the involvement of police and coroners is unavoidable. But thanks to the work of FSIDS there is now much greater public awareness of the issues involved and it is now less likely that the press will try to sensationalise these personal tragedies.

Stillbirths and neo-natal deaths

As little as ten years ago conventional wisdom dictated that the events of a stillbirth should be minimised; parents were advised to forget it as quickly as possible and to have another child. Little fuss was made. This was also the case until quite recently with miscarriages. Once the physical effects of a miscarriage were over, things were supposed to return to normal. But it seems that a great deal of silent grief has gone unattended; the Stillbirth and Neo-natal Death Society (SANDS) has campaigned for greater understanding of the problems parents face when they experience a miscarriage or stillbirth, and more and more parents are speaking out about their feelings and contacting SANDS for support. In legal terms, a baby born dead after 24 weeks of pregnancy is registered a stillbirth (until the Stillbirth (Definition) Act 1992 this was only after 28 weeks' gestation). There are certain procedures required by law. The stillbirth must be registered and certified and the body either buried or cremated. The parents' permission must be sought for any post mortem. The status of the baby is therefore acknowledged. Many hospitals have reviewed their procedures on stillbirths and there is a growing awareness among professionals of the needs of parents. The baby is no longer whisked away but parents are encouraged to hold and care for the body and are given time to say goodbye. Mementoes such as a lock of hair are given, or a photograph is taken. Many parents hold memorial services for their dead babies, and their loss is acknowledged as well as their need to mourn that loss.

A foetus of 23 weeks' gestation is not afforded any of this legal status but the attitudes and practices of hospital staff have changed with respect to miscarriages and parents of late miscarriages are often now given the same support as if it were legally a stillbirth, with the opportunity to hold the tiny foetus and bury or cremate it with some ceremony. SANDS maintains that this is helpful to parents, even if the foetus is damaged or abnormal, so long as they are given support from staff.

Early miscarriages can be just as traumatic as late ones. Most parents regard pregnancy in terms of the baby: they make plans, decide on names, speculate about whether it will be a boy or a girl, and worry about its development. Early miscarriage means the loss of all that that baby meant to them. It may have deeper significance; it may be the third miscarriage and so represent the loss of hope of becoming a parent at all. As Nancy Kohner, who writes on behalf of SANDS, says, 'It is the personal significance of the loss, not the gestational age of the baby, which determines the extent of parents' bereavement and their need to grieve.' But Nancy Kohner also cautions against assuming that every miscarriage will be experienced as deeply distressing. Not every pregnancy is invested with the same hopes and aspirations. There can be relief if the timing was not particularly good, or if an extra child would stretch an already tight budget, or if the pregnancy was not particularly welcomed for all manner of reasons. The level of care and support that professionals provide should be determined by an understanding of what the loss means to that particular set of parents, rather than by the stage the pregn.... had reached. Any guidelines on such care should always be tempered with an understanding of the individual parents involved, which makes it hard for professionals to know how to approach each set of parents. Nancy Kohner acknowledges this difficulty:

> *This means that to provide good care after loss at any stage in pregnancy, professionals must be able to listen and respond, as sensitively as they are able, to the feelings and needs of individual parents' experiences of loss and grief; the care and support they give should be determined by parents' particular needs. This means they must be prepared to work openly and flexibly, to communicate honestly with parents, to avoid assumptions and judgements, and sometimes, to risk making mistakes.*

(KOHNER 1993, P. 287)

She also goes on to say that given the challenging and demanding work that this is, professionals will need training and support themselves in what can be very harrowing work.

Bereavement after a terminal illness

In chapter 2 we discussed the issue of anticipatory grief and some of the effects on subsequent grief. The way that the actual death is experienced and the events surrounding it will have an effect on the bereaved person even though they may have been expecting it. For some people the death will represent the end of a struggle in which they may have been engaged with the dead person to combat the illness. The death could then be perceived as a failure and they will only now be coming to terms with it. They may be exhausted, mentally and physically. And if, after many months of caring for someone, they have had to allow that person to be admitted to hospital to die they may feel guilt and bitterness that they had not carried on for a while longer. How can hospital staff help to mitigate some of the pain of bereavement? In a booklet on good practice in hospital care for dying patients, Alix Henley (1986) points out that care of the dying person also involves care of the family and friends. She suggests the following ways in which staff can help before, at and immediately after the death.

Before the death

1 **Getting to know family and friends**
   At the time of the person's admission a member of staff should be made responsible for finding out about family and friends, for example, whether they have special needs perhaps to do with religious or cultural traditions, and how much they want to be involved. They should be considered part of the caring team.

2 **A key member of staff**
   One member of staff should have special responsibility for getting to know the relatives and friends well and making sure that they are kept informed and that they receive the care they need.

3 **Making relatives and friends feel welcome**
   When family or friends have been providing full-time care at home, the transition to hospital care can be difficult for them. They suddenly lose their role in the care of their loved one and hand over that responsibility to the hospital staff. To prevent feelings of failure, it can be helpful to offer them the chance to help with the day-to-day care of the dying person. They also have a lot of experience in caring for that individual which can be useful to hospital staff and should be valued. If they and the dying person agree, they should be allowed to stay while nursing and other procedures are carried out.

4 **Talking to relatives and friends in private**
   Although it is important to talk to dying people and their relatives together, there are times when relatives may wish to talk over their own anxieties in private and should be encouraged to approach staff if they need to do so.

5 **Keeping relatives and friends informed**
   Any developments in the dying person's condition should be

conveyed to the relatives and friends, particularly if death is imminent.

6 **Facilities for visitors**
People dying in hospital should be allowed 24-hour visiting if they wish. However, this can be exhausting for the dying person as well as for their relatives. Staff might suggest a break from the vigilance that some relatives impose upon themselves. But they should also ensure that the facilities for visitors are comfortable , having enough chairs by the bedside, access to refreshments and a telephone, and ideally a pleasantly furnished room where they can relax and talk privately. A room to stay overnight can be very helpful if they live a long way away or when death is imminent.

7 **Children of dying people**
Children should always be made welcome and allowed to visit freely, so that the death of someone close to them is not shrouded in mystery. Staff should be ready and willing to answer their questions as honestly and fully as possible.

8 **The language barrier**
If English is not the first language of the dying person or his/her relatives then an interpreter should be used so that everything is understood fully.

At the moment of death

1 **Calling relatives and friends**
The issue of whether relatives and friends want to be present when the person dies, even if this means calling them out at night, is best sorted out before the death. It should be clearly recorded in the person's notes so that night staff are aware of these wishes and know precisely whom to contact. The breaking of even expected bad news requires great sensitivity, especially if this happens over the telephone or at night.

2 **Accomodating different responses to death**
Enabling different religious and cultural practices at the time of

death to be carried out was discussed in chapter 7. This is as important for those left behind as it is for the person dying. You will recall the case of the death of Ramjit Sunil, described in chapter 2 (page 25), and the upset caused to his wife because she was not able to be with him when he died and the appropriate rituals were not observed.

When a person has just died

1 Sitting by the dead person
Bereaved people should be allowed to sit by the person who has died for as long as they wish. Privacy is important, even if it is only the drawing of curtains round the bed. Covering the face can be distressing and should be avoided; last offices should be left until after the bereaved have left. If for reasons of religion or culture there are specific people who should carry out these last offices then provision will have to be made for this.

2 Choosing not to see the person after death
Some people may prefer not to see or sit with the dead body and prefer to retain only live images. Finding out what people prefer to do rather than what they think is expected of them is not easy, but staff need to be sensitive to cues that people may convey and should make it clear that there is no 'right' way to behave.

3 Bereaved children
With children it is particularly important that they should neither be excluded from seeing or touching the dead person nor persuaded to do so if they are unwilling.

4 A cup of tea in private
The key member of staff who has looked after the dead person, if he or she is available, is the person who can probably give most comfort. He or she will be able to talk about the circumstances of the death and answer any queries. They may also have come to know the bereaved person quite well and so need time to say goodbye themselves.

5 **Explaining what will happen next**
Staff should give information regarding death certificates and the
registration of deaths; it is helpful if the hospital can provide a
simple and clear guide to these matters.

6 **The dead person's property**
A great deal of offence and unnecessary hurt can be caused by
insensitive handling of property. Thankfully the practice of using
black dustbin bags is now outlawed and suitable receptacles need
to be found. Flowers, half-used bottles of squash or boxes of
chocolates are best not included, although it is not always safe to
throw them away in case they are wanted. Valuables should be
listed and accounted for.

7 **Bereaved people who live alone**
Staff should check if a bereaved person is going back to an empty
house and perhaps offer to contact someone who can accompany
them. If there are no other relatives or friends then a hospital
visitor could be called upon.

Providing sensitive care to bereaved people can be very taxing and
staff will also need to be supported. Staff who have been caring for
someone for a long time before they died may have become
attached to them and also need to be allowed to grieve.

Hidden or forbidden grief

We often operate with the notion that it is only kin who grieve, but
the person closest to the dead person may not have kinship ties. The
term 'hidden' or 'forbidden' grief has been used to describe the
situation where a person's grief is not acknowledged.

Homosexual partners can sometimes feel left alone in their grief and
excluded by the family who are thought to be the legitimate
mourners. Sometimes this is deliberate, where the relationship was
not acknowledged or if the person died with AIDS and the family

are afraid of being stigmatised. These cases can be extremely distressing for the surviving partner, who badly needs the support and friendship of those who were also close to the person they loved.

Friends, particularly in adolescence, can be more important than family and their grief should always be acknowledged. Older people, especially older widows, form very close ties with other older women and acutely feel the loss of a much valued friend especially when it comes after other losses such as the loss of a spouse or a home. The following case study indicates how death in a residential home needs to be handled carefully.

— HIDDEN GRIEF IN A RESIDENTIAL HOME —

Emily James had been delighted when Rachel Davies came to live in Ash Grove residential home for older people. Emily had been in the home for about six months and she had been rather dismayed by the fact that most of the other residents were not very companionable. She wasn't unkind and was always willing to help, but there wasn't anyone with whom she could have a good conversation. A lot of the residents were confused and some were very deaf, which made it very hard to communicate. She was nearly ninety but was remarkably fit, apart from failing eyesight. It was this which had persuaded her to enter a home, because she was a widow and her only son lived in Canada and she wanted to get herself settled somewhere before she became heavily dependent. Rachel was 82 but couldn't walk far and had a bad heart. She had decided that she didn't want to live with her daughter and family because of the burdens that would impose, so she had sold her home and decided to move into Ash Grove. She and Emily struck up a friendship almost immediately. They discovered that they had a lot in common and shared a passion for gardening. Emily pushed Rachel around the grounds in the summer and Rachel compensated for Emily's poor eyesight by pointing out and describing the different plants in the garden. They took over the conservatory and created quite a tropical atmosphere there. Sadly, about nine months after entering the home Rachel had a heart attack and died in the night. The officer in charge came into Emily's room at about eight in the morning to tell her the sad news. She knew that this was going to be a blow for Emily and tried to break the news as kindly as possible. Emily was shocked and very upset but she asked if she could go and see Rachel's body and say goodbye to her. Unfortunately it was the home's policy that if a death occurred in the night the night staff arranged for the undertaker to remove the body as soon as possible before the other residents get up. They thought that this protected the other residents from having to face death. As Rachel's family all lived a long way away it was not possible for Emily to attend her funeral – and anyway, nobody thought to ask her. She felt bereft and very much as she did when her husband died. She kept telling herself that she shouldn't feel so bad; after all, Rachel wasn't family and she had only known her for nine months. But the feeling didn't go away. She couldn't face going into the conservatory and spent most of her time in her own room listening to the radio, which was her only pleasure.

In the context of her present life Emily's loss was considerable; but her need to grieve was not acknowledged, she was not able to express it or to share it with anyone else. Because most deaths occur in old age and a proportion of older people live in residential homes especially when they are frail and in extreme old age, death is not an infrequent event. Yet the staff in such homes are often unsure of how to approach the issues and sometimes tend to deny death, especially if they are trying to create a cheerful and optimistic atmosphere. The inclination is to conceal death and therefore the dying person, and not to dwell upon grief. This can result in less than sensitive care for anyone who dies in the home. Moreover, companions like Emily are not allowed to grieve. Rachel's death could have been marked by some event; this need not have been a morbid occasion but could on the contrary have been a celebration of her life which Emily might like to have organised in the conservatory. This would have established and recognised her loss.

In this chapter we have been concentrating on the events surrounding a death and the immediate impact of bereavement. In the next chapter we look first at the impact of the funeral and then at the longer-term aspects of grief and mourning.

9

Supporting bereaved people through the mourning process

In chapter 5 we discussed three components of support: emotional, cognitive or informational, and instrumental or practical. In this chapter we will focus on these three components to explore ways of supporting people in their grief.

Emotional support

We may not readily associate the giving of emotional support with professional carers, but in the last chapter we identified times when such support might be appropriate from professionals. The word empathy was used to indicate the need to show that one understood the depth of feeling that a bereaved person might be experiencing. Finding the right word or gesture to convey that empathy is not easy. It can mean indicating that it is all right to show emotion openly and being prepared to absorb and share some of that emotion. Touching is a sensitive issue; it may be welcomed, it may not be. Offering a hand in warmth and friendship or a comforting arm around the shoulders may be valued by one person but perceived by another as an intrusion into private grief. Much will depend on the particular circumstances and on how well the carer knows the bereaved person.

Very often people give cues as to how they would like to be treated. Being observant and alert to those cues can be gained through appropriate training; we should not expect professionals to know automatically how to deal with such highly charged situations. Bob

Wright, who has made a study of nurses' reactions to bereaved people, points out how harrowing it can be to 'witness and share another person's extremes of anguish and distress' (1989, p. 3). But from his research with relatives who were suddenly bereaved he indicates how much they valued the 'personal touch' that some nurses managed to bring. He writes: 'It is our own personal touch, our own humanity, that is experienced by relatives in these situations. They remember many personal details about us. If your role, experience or expertise appears to have little to offer, or you feel ineffective or impotent, do not be afraid to fall back on your own personal skills, your own humanity. People remember with warmth, and are grateful for, the person they meet on that awful day' (1989, p. 4).

Cognitive or informational support

Cognitive support, the giving of advice and information, may be more straightforward. This may include giving advice about how to claim a death benefit, how to register a death and obtain a death certificate. Information may be needed about any post mortem procedures which are necessary; or the names and addresses of appropriate self-help agencies may be useful. People who are in a state of shock may not easily be able to take in such information and again sensitivity is needed in judging how much information to give to people and in what form: for instance, it may help to write down the names and addresses of certain organisations which you may be recommending they contact. If there is not a shared language then it may be necessary to obtain the services of an interpreter. Another form of informational support which is very much appreciated by bereaved people is the information about the actual death of their loved one. This will be especially valued if the bereaved person was not present at the death. They may not like to ask, but would probably like to know whether the dead person suffered, how aware he or she was, whether he or she said anything, and so on. They may also like to know about the medical cause of death and what treatments were tried, if they do not already know about this.

Instrumental or practical support

This kind of support is typically provided by friends, family or work colleagues. But not everyone has a social network on whom to call. An older widowed man may have lost his cook as well as his wife and companion. Arranging for meals on wheels or introducing him to a luncheon club might help keep him well nourished as well as providing him with some company. Sometimes it is only through doing something practical, such as taking someone on a weekly shopping trip, that the opportunity is provided to build up the trust which is necessary for someone to accept emotional or informational support which they may need.

Supporting people through the mourning process

Grief can be defined as the emotional response to loss, and mourning is the outward expression of that grief. There are two major components to mourning: one is the inner feelings associated with grief and the other is the social convention of expected behaviour. Certain types of behaviour are expected of bereaved people; these have changed over time and they vary now according to religion and culture. It is generally thought that in western culture there has been a decline in mourning rituals and that this makes grieving more difficult. So what is it about mourning rituals that may aid the process of grieving? Most rituals allow for people to show emotion, to express their grief and provide a socially acceptable framework for grief. They are a public recognition of the death and affirm the loss. They allow the bereaved time off from their normal duties to experience the loss. They ensure social support for the bereaved. They provide 'milestones' over a period of time which allow the bereaved gradually to let go of the dead person and to adapt to change. And some provide an end point to the mourning when things are supposed to return to normal.

Funerals

Funerals provide an acceptable way of disposing of the body and in some cultures for aiding the transition into other states. They also act as a protection from experiencing grief too intensely by giving people something to get on with; the organisation of the funeral can in itself be therapeutic. Funerals are an important landmark in the mourning process; some people dread them, others find them comforting. Some people only come to realise the reality of their loss at the funeral, others are only able to start to heal when they have buried or cremated their loved one. But either way the funeral is likely to be a sensitive time for a bereaved person. They may be anxious about how they should behave, what to wear, how much overt grief they ought to display. Some people find it hard to display grief in public but fear condemnation if they seem to be unaffected. They may also be extremely sensitive to the behaviour of others. The numbers who attend the funeral can be significant, indicating the degree of respect paid to the dead person. Sometimes people attend who are not welcome, yet others who do not attend are sadly missed, leaving bereaved people feeling neglected or even resentful. The funeral can be experienced as a supportive occasion which will be remembered positively or a bleak and barren affair which leaves a scar for some time to come. Some people feel more comfortable with set rituals, others like the freedom to organise the funeral in their own way.

Mourning rituals are strongest where religion and cultural identity are important. As Britain has become a more secular society and local communities have become more fragmented, so too have mourning rituals declined. But for those who do practise a particular religion it is important that they be able to carry out the rituals associated with their religion. We have discussed in previous chapters the religious practices relating to dying and the preparation of the body for disposal. Now we need to review the mourning rituals of those who do practise a particular religion and the implications for providing social support. If professionals are to offer appropriate support then it is important to understand what is and is not acceptable.

Buddhists can either bury or cremate the body and a service is usually held in the house before going on to the cemetery or crematorium. At the service the emphasis will be on the impermanence of life. Mourning traditions vary according to the country of origin: some Buddhists will return to work within three or four days with no special restrictions on widows, whereas Vietnamese Buddhists mourn for up to 100 days and women mourn their husbands or fathers for up to three years.

Muslims like to bury their dead within 24 hours of death. Only male members officiate at the burial, at which the body is buried in a deep grave facing Mecca. Muslims would prefer to bury their dead in a shroud without the coffin but there are restrictions on this in Britain. Some Muslims like to embalm the bodies and take them back to the country of origin. Friends and relatives are required to provide instrumental support to the mourners by feeding them for three days, which is the official mourning period; but mourning is finally ended after 40 days by readings from the Qur'an and a special meal.

Hindus and Sikhs always cremate. Both hold a short ceremony in the home before going to the crematorium. Sikh bodies are always dressed in their sacred symbols, the 5Ks. After the cremation mourners and friends return to the home. A period of mourning lasts around ten days, during which relatives and friends visit and readings from the scriptures are given. There may be further rituals at one, three and six months, and finally at twelve months to mark the end of the mourning period.

Like Islam, Judaism specifies burial, although some non-Orthodox Jews choose cremation. Burial takes place in a Jewish cemetery and male mourners recite prayers and place the coffin in the grave. For the first week after a death, those who are obliged to mourn remain at home and pray three times a day. They are visited by relatives and friends. Mourning is concluded at the end of 30 days, except for children of the deceased who mourn for a year.

Christians either bury or cremate. For most Christians the funeral involves a church service sometimes with a mass or communion. The body is then taken to the crematorium or burial ground where further prayers are said over the coffin. Very little has survived of the mourning rituals which used to be common, such as wearing certain types of clothing; but some traditions are still observed in the north of England and in Ireland, where wakes are held which provide mourners with some emotional support from friends and relatives.

Those who do not belong to any organised religion have generally used the facilities of the state religion for such ceremonies as marriages and deaths. But many have found the performance of rituals which have little significance for them a most unsatisfactory way of marking the death of someone they love. Until quite recently it has been hard to organise a satisfactory funeral without resorting to the church. But the British Humanist Society has published a booklet, *Funerals without God* (1989), which provides information and guidance on how to conduct a funeral, and there is a growing network of people who will conduct a non-religious funeral. The most important purposes of a humanist funeral are to remember the dead and pay tribute to the life that has ended; it is a summing up of the character and life of an individual. It is thus a celebration of that person's life. People pay tribute to the dead person, read appropriate pieces of literature and play favourite pieces of music. They are intensely personal affairs and so can be very moving occasions. It is becoming more common now for dying people to request certain features for their own funerals.

Professional carers may be asked whether children should attend the funeral. Much will depend on the age of the child, the relationship to the dead person and family traditions. Funerals can help children to acknowledge that a change has taken place and that other people share in the loss and value the dead person. But they do need information on what to expect and they should be given the choice to attend or not to attend.

The question of whether professional carers should attend funerals is a difficult one. Where cultural or religious traditions dictate who should and should not attend then it is important that these should here are often many practical reasons which make it impossible for professionals to attend funerals, yet they may have become very close to the dead person over a long period in hospital and would like to pay their respects. Even if they have the opportunity they may feel they would be intruding on a private and family occasion; but their presence can be very supportive to mourners, especially if they have been closely involved with the death. Hospices usually as a matter of policy try to send a key professional carer to a funeral. Sending flowers or messages of sympathy is almost always much appreciated by bereaved people.

After the funeral

The period after the funeral is often difficult for a bereaved person. Up to that time there will have been lots to do, and probably a lot of people expressing their condolences and support, emotional, cognitive and instrumental. Then everyone else's life goes back to normal; yet for someone bereaved their life can be totally changed and they can feel very alone with their loss. This is a time when a follow-up visit or phone call from the hospital or hospice can be a lifeline. Knowing how or when to intervene and offer professional help to a bereaved person is difficult. But a visit or telephone call, especially if it is from someone who nursed or was involved with the dead person in some capacity, will usually be welcomed and it provides the opportunity to assess the situation. Most people will have adequate support networks and, however sad their loss, will not need professional help. But some people do not have very good support networks and there are some situations which may give cause for concern. Certain 'risk factors' have been identified which might indicate that someone could benefit from professional help. These can be grouped under three headings, as shown opposite.

FACTORS WHICH INDICATE A PERSON MIGHT BENEFIT FROM PROFESSIONAL HELP

Factors which predate the loss

- Poor mental or physical health. This can be exacerbated by the loss.

- Personality. Anxious, fearful and insecure individuals are likely to react badly to bereavement

- A difficult or heavily dependent relationship with the dead person. Difficult relationships can result in feelings of ambivalence which in turn create guilt which can be hard to deal with. When someone has lost someone on whom they were heavily dependent, they lose not only that person but their own sense of security.

Factors associated with the loss

- Sudden and unexpected deaths are thought to be particularly difficult to deal with especially if the bereaved person has feelings of guilt associated with things they did or did not say or do.

- Loss of a child. Parents who lose a child often say that they feel as though they have lost part of themselves, they have lost part of their future. They also experience a loss of confidence in their ability to protect their child, however irrational that may be.

- Loss due to suicide. This leaves so many questions unanswered and also many 'if onlys' which lead to feelings of guilt.

Circumstances after the loss

- Concurrent loss of financial security or loss of a home. Widows often experience such financial losses and older widows are among the poorest members of our society.

- Lack of social support from family or friends. Having no one to turn to or to talk to means that there is no one to share one's grief. Having a confidant can be a great help in bereavement; the lack of this can result in social isolation which in turn can lead to depression.

- Family discord or tensions. Even when there is a family available this does not mean that members will be able to share their feelings and provide the support that each of them may need. They may in fact serve only to remind each other of the loss and feel guilty about each other. Bereaved parents can find that they reach a state of exhaustion when they can no longer give each other the support they need when they need it.

- Concurrent crisis. This may result from multiple deaths, perhaps due to a road accident, or when one death follows fairly soon after another. But another crisis may occur around the time of bereavement, such as loss of job or failure to gain promotion. This can stretch the individual's resources too far.

These factors are only indicators of possible difficulties which may require professional support, and each person will react in different ways. Some people will resent professional help and see it as an intrusion; others would welcome it but might not know how to seek such help. There are now many different organisations which offer help and support to bereaved people: some are specifically for bereaved parents, others for those bereaved by specific types of death, such as the Stillbirth and Neo-natal Death Society; yet others are available for the whole range of bereavements. They all provide leaflets giving information on the type of service they can offer and telephone contact numbers. It is useful for hospitals, health centres and doctors surgeries to keep a stock of this material so that they can at least alert bereaved people to the help that is available. Many of these organisations are run by people who have themselves been bereaved, especially bereaved parents, and so they are able to understand the feelings that are likely to be experienced.

One-to-one counselling is available from a range of organisations, some statutory, some voluntary. Anyone who offers counselling will have undergone some training in counselling skills. The general aim of counselling is to allow the bereaved person to talk through their feelings and to work through their grief. Worden's work (1983) on grief counselling and grief therapy has been very influential in shaping much bereavement counselling. It mirrors quite closely the stages of grief and reactions to loss which we discussed in chapter 2. Worden claims that there are four tasks of mourning, as shown below.

WORDEN'S FOUR TASKS OF MOURNING

Task 1 is to accept the reality of the loss, to come to terms with the shock and disbelief that is very common immediately after a bereavement.

Task 2 is to experience the pain of grief. Giving vent to anger and acknowledging the pain is considered to be cathartic.

Task 3 is to adjust to an environment from which the deceased is missing. Worden believes that feelings of anxiety and helplessness and loss of self-confidence have to be dealt with if the bereaved person is to overcome their grief.

Task 4 is to withdraw emotional energy from the lost person and reinvest it in another relationship or activity.

However, most bereavement counsellors do not work to any rigid framework and accept that people grieve in different ways. They do not put time limits on these stages or tasks, but see their role as supporting the person in whatever ways they feel appropriate to the situation. Some counsellors, though, do work out counselling contracts with their clients and agree to a certain number of sessions over a period of time. The last of Worden's tasks has caused a certain amount of controversy, with many bereaved people seeing this as inappropriate. We will return to the issue of facing the future later in this chapter.

Befriending or bereavement visiting is a form of support which is perhaps not so intense as actual counselling. The aim is to provide social contact and friendlike behaviour for someone who is lonely and socially isolated. The visitor may also have experienced a similar bereavement and therefore can empathise with the person's feelings.

Telephone helplines are usually run by self-help groups such as SANDS, FSIDS or Compassionate Friends; they try to provide 24-hour cover so that they are available at difficult times for people, such as in the night. They can be used in a range of circumstances. They can provide emotional help in a crisis when someone feels that they have reached the end of their tether, or they can provide informational help such as advising someone about the best way to dispose of a loved one's clothing.

There is also group therapy, which can range from the more formal closed group, lasting for about six weekly sessions and run by a trained facilitator, to an open, regular group which may have a professional facilitator or may be run by volunteers who have been bereaved. Some organisations also run weekly drop-in sessions which are more social occasions providing company and comradeship.

As you read through the following three short case vignettes, try to decide which, if any, of the services described above might benefit the bereaved people.

——— EXPERIENCES OF BEREAVEMENT ———

Rosemary and Jim Wright's son, Tim, was knocked off his cycle by a lorry which turned a corner while Tim was in its blind spot. He was rushed to hospital but died from head injuries. He was just 14. He had a younger sister Linda who was ten. Rosemary had always hated the fact that Tim cycled everywhere but Jim had encouraged it, saying that she was over-protective and he ought to be more independent. Linda was coming up for her 11th birthday and had been putting a lot of pressure on her mother to let her have a bicycle too so that she could join her friends on Saturdays instead of having to be taken everywhere by her mother. Rosemary now said that this was out of the question and so Linda's grief for her brother was tinged with resentment that what she suspected was probably carelessness on Tim's part had caused such a lot of tension in the family. She had never seen her mother so distraught and she had also heard some unpleasant rows between her parents. Rosemary was blaming Jim for the accident because, as she argued, if it had been up to her Tim would not have been on a cycle at all. Jim felt desolate about his son's death and although he resented Rosemary's inferences he still had his own guilt to deal with.

Norma and Allan Bury had taken early retirement and moved to live in a cottage on the coast. The cottage had a big garden because that was Allan's main hobby. They had two grown-up sons who were married and had small families, but neither lived locally. They had lived there for about a year when Allan was diagnosed as having cancer of the pancreas, and within six months he was dead. Norma had nursed him through his illness which had been quite a harrowing experience because he had become very bad-tempered and very difficult to nurse, insisting that he would beat it even to the last. She was exhausted and felt numb at the funeral. Her sons inhibited her from showing any emotion, saying 'You've got to be brave, mum, for the rest of the family.' After the funeral she had gone back to the cottage but could not sleep and felt agitated most of the day, not able to relax but not able to face doing anything either. She went to her GP who gave her sleeping pills and some tranquillisers for the day which she was glad of. Then the bills started to come in. Theirs had been a traditional marriage; Allan had taken care of all the financial matters and she had been glad to let him do so. Now she had to sort it all out and it seemed that his pension was much diminished. It looked as though she couldn't afford to live in the cottage and anyway she didn't know how she would cope with the garden. But the thought of moving was equally daunting. She felt she was living in a fog, not knowing what she might bump into next. She didn't like to bother her sons because they had their own families, and she and Allan had not made any close friends since they had moved.

Dick Chester was 82 and had buried two wives in the last three years. His first wife's death had been a massive blow but he had been determined to get over it and then when he met Maria, who was also widowed, he was amazed that at 79 he had found such happiness. Now that she too had died he felt that it had been some cruel joke or that somehow he was tainted with death. He withdrew into himself, didn't eat and didn't care whether he lived or died. He didn't reply to the GP's offer of an over-75s health check and was quite rude to the local vicar when he called soon after the funeral.

Of these three cases, Norma Bury is perhaps the easiest person to help. A bereavement visitor would be able to befriend her, allow her to talk over her feelings and anxieties, and suggest that she try to take fewer tranquillisers, especially in the daytime, so that her mind would feel clearer. A bereavement visitor could also provide her with informational help on how to sort out her finances and perhaps accompany her to the Citizen's Advice Bureau, thus providing a degree of emotional and instrumental support as well.

It's hard to know where to start with the Wright family. One way would be to try to get Rosemary to accept one-to-one bereavement counselling, in the hope that if she could feel less resentful towards her husband they would be able to help each other – and Linda, who was left with very conflicting emotions. Another approach might be to get them both to join a bereaved parents' support group, where they would meet others who would have encountered similar situations and where they would be able to talk through their difficulties in a supportive atmosphere. Other parents would also have experience of dealing with other children, and so might help them to understand Linda's needs as well.

Dick Chester looks like a very difficult person to help. He has so far rejected any overtures from his doctor or vicar. A telephone or letter from the hospital where his second wife died inviting him to drop in to one of their weekly coffee mornings and perhaps including a leaflet about a local telephone helpline would at least show that people cared about him but were not thrusting themselves upon him. Then he would have the information to enable him to take up offers of help if he decided he wanted to.

Offering help to people in their grief can be problematic. They may well reject it, or they may accept help and then find that it does not meet their particular needs and feel disappointed. The full range of bereavement support we have discussed here is not available in all areas, and appropriate help may just not be on offer. There is also the issue that grief can be overprofessionalised and overmedicalised and that people will find their own ways of facing the future.

Facing the future, remembering the past

One of the functions of mourning rituals is that they provide a framework for mourning and prescribe a time limit on how long the mourning phase should last. The stages model of grief which has become so widely accepted in western culture also sets an end point for grief, with the last stage, 'reintegration and reorganisation', representing a move into a new life. Time limits have also been put on reaching that stage although over the years these have become something of a moving target. Rituals represent a public manifestation of grief which may not mirror an individual's private feelings; in much the same way, the stages model of grief describes a process with which many people can identify, although their own personal experience may not match the model precisely. It is when the model becomes a blueprint for acceptable behaviour that there is cause for concern. The expectation that after a certain number of years a bereaved person will have 'got over' their grief and be making a new life for him/herself can be an imposition to someone who still feels their loss acutely and who has no desire to start a new life. Many bereaved people resent the implication that they should not dwell on the past and on the dead person. Keeping the memory alive is very important to some bereaved people. Yet prolonged grief and such dwelling on the past has in some instances been interpreted as indicating abnormality or pathology. However, more and more bereaved people are speaking out about their experiences and indicating that they go on enduring grief for a long time, possibly all their lives, however hard other people might find this to accept. As you read the following case studies, reflect on the notion of what is normal and what is abnormal about them.

━━━━━━━━━ GRIEVING FOR EMMA ━━━━━━━━━

It is three years since Gwen's youngest daughter Emma was run over and killed just outside her home at the age of two and a half, yet Gwen bakes a cake each year on Emma's birthday. Those three years have been a difficult time for all involved. Initially Peter, her husband, was a tower of strength.

Gwen's mother took the other two children, a girl of seven and a boy of five, to live with her initially for about a month to give Gwen and Peter some space in which to grieve. Gwen was glad of Peter's support and left everything to him while she tried to cope with not only the pain of her loss but also her feelings of guilt that she should have somehow prevented it. The catch on the front door was faulty and the door had blown open soon after she had brought the milk in. Her daughter had ventured outside and on to the road in a trice. Gwen had replayed those moments over and over in her mind, especially at night as she lay only fitfully sleeping. Peter was a teacher, and because the accident occured in the second week of the summer holidays he was able to be at home for the first month. He was worried as the new school term approached because Gwen was very withdrawn and listless and he didn't know how he was going to cope with the other two children and a busy term as well. Gwen's mother agreed to keep the other children for a little while longer, but Peter began to feel that Gwen was neglecting her duty to them and he was beginning to feel exhausted by it all. His own grief was somehow not acknowledged, although he too missed their daughter a great deal. He felt that Gwen denied him the right to grieve because when they had first learnt that Gwen was pregnant with their third child he was less than enthusiastic. They already had a 'perfect' family, a boy and a girl. Things weren't easy financially and he was hoping that Gwen, who was also a trained teacher, would soon return to work, if only part-time, to ease the financial strain. He had left the contraception to her and was angry that she had slipped up. It had been a difficult time, but they had managed to get over it and there was no doubt in his mind that their youngest daughter was much loved. Now all the bitterness came back and he felt the unspoken accusation of Gwen, who seemed to move further and further away from him.

Gwen's mother could see that her daughter's family was in danger of falling apart and she felt helpless. However, she had heard of various bereavement organisations and decided to make some enquiries to find out what was available in their area. She found out that there was a bereavement support group for parents not too far away and she managed to persaude Gwen to go on the basis that she could talk to other parents who had been through similar bereavements. This appealed to Gwen, who, although she had isolated herself from her husband, still felt a great need to talk about her grief. Meeting with other parents enabled Gwen to voice her resentment against her husband and talk about the barriers that had built up since their daughter's death. She discovered that for a whole range of reasons other couples had experienced similar difficulties, some had overcome them, some had not. What she valued most about the group was that she could talk openly about her dead daughter without people trying to change the subject or thinking she was morbid or dwelling on her grief. She was relieved to find that, far from trying to forget their loss, the emphasis was on keeping the memory alive. She found that other people celebrated the birthdays of their dead children too and would often say such things as 'Julie would be going to secondary school now' or 'Simon would have loved to have learnt to canoe'. She had been dreading her daughter's third birthday, but now she decided to make a cake and take it to the group meeting. She was touched to find that they had anticipated this and had sent her a card to mark her daughter's birthday. Having somewhere to talk about her daughter and celebrate her life enabled Gwen to cope with the rest of her life. The other children were back home and she was beginning to think about returning to work; she started to make some enquiries about supply teaching. She decided to do a refresher course first as she felt a little unconfident about returning to the classroom after such a gap.

Two years later Gwen started teaching full-time after working part-time for a year. She still makes a cake for Emma's birthday, which she shares with two other parents she met in the group who are now her firm friends. They always remember each other's dead children's birth and death days, and they share their lost hopes and aspirations. Sadly she is not able to share this with her own family, because she thinks they will think she is dwelling on the past; but for Gwen this enables her to face the future.

On the face of it making birthday cakes for dead children might seem a little irrational, but within the context of her group it is understandable behaviour. The issue is not that she does this but that her family cannot accept that it is a legitimate way of remembering something precious.

REKINDLED GRIEF

Mrs Weale was widowed in her early fifties when her husband died suddenly from a heart attack. This was a blow to her, not only because she lost her husband and companion but because they lost their hopes for their future retirement which they had both been looking forward to. Mr Weale had been a skilled tradesman all his life and had made good provision for his pension. Mrs Weale also worked and although this was part-time and did not attract pensionable benefits she had managed to save quite a bit for their retirement. They had also bought a small semi-detached house on which they had finished the mortgage payments, and so, from having struggled to bring up a family of three, they were set for a comfortable retirement. It had been a painful process for Mrs Weale to adjust to a life without her husband and without the future that they had planned together. She had good support from her three children, who were launching themselves into careers and marriages. Mrs Weale worked at Marks and Spencers and they were very good about allowing her compassionate leave and encouraging her to come back to work when she was ready. She found the companionship at work particularly helpful, and she found that she got quite close to one or two women who were also widowed. She also spent a lot of time with her daughter's children who lived in the same town; she was fit and healthy and had good friends and family. She missed Bill, of course; his picture remained by her bedside and she often thought about him and what they might have done.

Mrs Weale had adjusted to her widowhood and made a full life for herself. She retired at 60 but still enjoyed a busy social life. But by her early seventies she started to suffer quite badly from osteoarthritis in her knees. Eventually she was put on the waiting list for an operation but over a period of two years her knees got so bad that her mobility was severely restricted. Added to this, her daughter, who used to live in the same town, had moved three years ago to Wales and so now all her children lived a train journey away. They came to visit her and took her to stay with them but she found it hard to keep up with their growing families and so tended to stay at home and became more isolated. More and more she thought about Bill, how lovely it would be to have someone close, to be there to share her life, someone to talk to and share her anxieties about her operation. She talks to his picture now, she frequently dreams about him and finds that she misses him again just as much as she did when he first died, which was over 20 years ago.

As well as enduring, for some people, like Mrs Weale, grief can be rekindled. It is not difficult to imagine that when physical frailty restricts one's life and renders one housebound the loss of a spouse can be felt acutely again even after many years and even when one thought the loss had been adjusted to.

———————— MATTHEW LEVER ————————

Some days Matthew Lever could still not believe that his wife was dead. As he was an Orthodox Jew and they had no children the requirement to attend the synagogue each day had fallen on him. Now, one year later, that was no longer necessary. Life was supposed to return to normal. But what was normal he wondered? He was a man on his own, no ties, free to do what he wanted. He was young, in his mid-thirties, and a successful businessman. Most people assumed he would remarry soon, but that thought was repugnant to him. The thought of replacing Miriam would be a betrayal of everything she had meant to him. He was in fact rather resentful that he was no longer required to attend the synagogue each day. He admitted that once or twice he had found the daily attendance irksome, especially after a late meeting, but that daily observance had given meaning to the last year, it had been the focus of his life. Somehow it had meant that his life was still bound up with hers. Now it was finished. What was so special about a year, he thought? He still missed her as much after a year and a day, a year and three months, a year and six months. He couldn't imagine a time when he would not miss her. Yet no one else talked about her, indeed they avoided the subject. Clearly everyone thought he should be over the worst. Friends started to invite him to parties and introduce him to people, seeing him as an available man. So he declined most invitations and when he did, his family told him that this was no way to carry on, that he had to rebuild his life. But he wanted to keep the memory of her alive; he was somehow frightened that the images would fade and that he would no longer be able to recall her voice and facial expressions.

Matthew's own need to mourn outlasted the public requirement and he resented the expectation that he should be 'over' his grief. As we noted earlier, the public expression of grief through mourning rituals does not necessarily match the personal grief that is felt by an individual. For this reason attempts to mould grief into a set pattern or prescribe the limits of normal behaviour are to be avoided. On the other hand, some people are comforted if they know what to expect and what they can expect of others, and many people want some reassurance that the pain of grief will not go on for ever. Also, we know from studies such as the work of Colin Murray Parkes that grief can render people vulnerable to ill-health, particularly mental ill-health. If we are saying that people should be allowed to grieve in their own way, when should we be worried about a bereaved person's health? I would not think that Gwen, Mrs Weale or Matthew was in particular need of psychiatric help but there might be other forms of support that might be helpful. In Gwen's case it could be argued that there were some unresolved conflicts between her and her husband. On the other hand, she had evolved a way of living with her own grief that enabled her to cope with her life. Mrs Weale probably would have benefited from some regular company. Matthew might benefit from counselling, perhaps even group therapy, where he could talk about his dead wife uninhibitedly and in an atmosphere which encouraged this. In a more general sense we would need to be worried about someone's mental state if they showed signs of depression or expressed suicidal thoughts, or perhaps if they showed some form of physical distress such as loss of weight or extreme fatigue.

Wanting to keep the memory of a dead loved one alive seems to be important to many bereaved people. Resolving or coming to terms with grief is not about forgetting, and many bereaved people share a need to talk and reminisce about the dead person, particularly with someone who also knew that person. Too often that need is denied them in the belief that they have to look to the future and forget the past. Yet most of us hope that our own memory will live on after our death in the minds of those we have been close to, and for some people that is the only form of immortality that they will accept.

10

Conclusions

In this book we have been exploring how to improve the quality of care for dying and bereaved people.

We have made a historical and cultural analysis of how care for dying and bereaved people has evolved in Britain today; but this is not a theoretical book, and through the extensive use of case study material we have tried to focus on the experience of death and dying in contemporary Britain, and have used a problem-solving approach to the dilemmas of caring for dying and bereaved people. In this final chapter we want to draw together some of the themes and dilemmas that have emerged throughout the book.

Looking at the past

A familiar theme nowadays is that, compared to other times and other cultures, death and dying are handled badly in modern Britain. People avoid the subject of death and dying, and so dying and bereaved people are neglected and unsupported when they are particularly vulnerable. Various reasons have been suggested for this. One is demographic – ironically, a result of the success of western societies in increasing life expectancy. The experience of death, compared to other times, is concentrated in the old age group. Death and dying are unfamiliar events. Added to this there has been a structural change in the nature of the family, with smaller and more geographically mobile families, leading to less availablilty of people to care for dying people at home. This is connected to another of the reasons put forward to explain why death is an alien event. It is said that death has become medicalised and professionalised, and so removed from everyday life. Advances in medical science have achieved much in saving lives and so death is seen as a preventable and a medical event; therefore dying is considered a failure. This has meant that most deaths take place in hospitals in the care of professional people. As western societies have become more secularised many of the rituals and familiar practices involved in death and dying have faded away, although in contrast multi-cultural societies such as Britain now incorporate many different groups of people with distinct rituals and practices.

To many of these arguments there are counter-arguments. Many would claim that the rise of the hospice movement and the advances in palliative care have greatly improved the care of dying and bereaved people, and that medical and professional people have much to offer. Arguments abound about the breakdown of the family and its changing nature. But although most people actually die in hospitals, most of their care is provided by informal carers. The absence of ritual in modern societies can be seen as a mark of individual freedom, with ritual portrayed as a constraint. Clearly the issues are far from clear-cut and there are many dilemmas involved in providing the care of dying and bereaved people.

Looking at the present

Dilemmas of disclosure

We have stressed the value of good communication between dying people and their carers, and the importance of honesty. But openness and honesty are not always unproblematic. Telling someone that they have a terminal illness, that their life is about to end sooner rather than later, is one of the most difficult things that a health worker may have to do. Much has been written about sensitive ways of doing this, and there is much that can be learnt. It seems that most people want to know the truth about their condition; but it is by no means safe to assume that this is always the case. The dilemma of disclosure lies in gauging how much the person wants to know and when, as well as how, to tell them. Honesty is also compromised in the face of uncertainty. A diagnosis of a terminal illness rarely provides a clear-cut prognosis and uncertainty can be very hard to handle.

Dilemmas of providing support

We have talked a lot in this book about providing support to dying and bereaved people. But there are dilemmas here about how much support and of what kind can be expected of a professional carer.

Getting involved and providing emotional support can have huge costs for professionals which may adversely affect their ability to carry on. How many people can one give that kind of support at any one time, and for how long? Death and dying are personal as well as professional issues. How does caring for dying and bereaved people affect a professional's personal life? What if they have a death in their own intimate circle? Will they have enough emotional energy to cope at home as well as at work? We have strongly advocated in this book that professionals engaged in this work need care and support themselves, which might include counselling and one-to-one help. The issue is also one about resources. Having adequate staffing levels, good pay and good working conditions, being able to take breaks and afford holidays and having the time and money to engage in leisure pursuits are also important. Having their work valued and recognised, not just by individual dying and bereaved people but by society as a whole, is vital for professional carers.

However, providing emotional support is not only a matter of the impact on carers. We cannot always assume that it will be welcomed by dying and bereaved people, although there is a great deal of evidence to suggest that many people are helped a great deal by an empathetic gesture. It is not easy to gauge how much support and of what kind a dying or bereaved person wants or will accept from a professional carer who may be a total stranger. Displays of warmth and affection inappropriately made can be offensive to some people and may provoke rejection.

Physical contact can be unacceptable for reasons of religion or culture. We have tried to give guidance in this book on the various religious and cultural traditions which are likely to be encountered in Britain today. But here too making assumptions can be dangerous. There is great diversity within each religion and culture, and many of the traditions have become eroded or adapted to life in Britain. In all of these areas professionals need to be sensitive to individual differences.

Individual differences in reactions to grief are also important if appropriate support is to be given to bereaved people. Holding fixed ideas on what is normal or abnormal behaviour in bereavement can be unhelpful. Not everyone who is bereaved needs help, and imposing too much support can be overwhelming. On the other hand, withdrawing support because it is 'time the person had got over their grief' is to force their grief into an accepted mould which may not match their own feelings.

There are many pitfalls and dilemmas in caring for dying and bereaved people; but there are also great opportunities, and it is an area of work that can give immense satisfaction, given adequate resources.

Looking to the future

Have we reached the limits of the human life-span? Some argue that we have, and that the natural span is about ten years more than three score and ten. This puts the average life at about 80 to 85. As this is an average, then the range can reach to 100 and even 110. Those who argue that we have not reached the limits of natural life-span point to the growing numbers of 100 and 110-year-olds as evidence that the average human life-span could reach 100. Advances in medical science and improvements in living standards have had dramatic effects on life expectancy, and this is generally thought of as an advance. What worries many people is the ability to prolong life after it has ceased to be experienced as meaningful, even tolerable. Many

Conclusions

would argue that this is merely prolonging suffering and is not a health gain.

As we discussed in the first chapter, it is not so much death itself which people fear but the manner in which they will die, and many dread being kept alive in pain or in a vegetative state, no pleasure to themselves and a burden to others. This has been the impetus behind the campaigns to make voluntary euthanasia legal in this Britain. So far these campaigns have not been successful in spite of a good deal of public support. But the latest recommendation from the British Medical Association's Ethics Committee considering these matters took seriously the anxieties of people and recommended that emphasis should be given to attempts to improve palliative care and that the practice of good palliative care should be available to everyone. This is by no means the case now, with hospice provision patchy and terminal care in hospitals of greatly varying quality.

The training of health professionals in palliative care is important if the quality of dying is to be improved, as is the availability of resources generally. Although almost everyone agrees that palliative care should be widely available, there is competition for scarce health service resources. Unless palliative care is given a high priority then the overall quality of dying will not be improved.

One of the recommendations of the BMA ethics committee was that 'living wills' or 'advance directives' should become legal documents. This would enable people to make choices about their own terminal care and make clear to professional carers what these preferences are. If these documents are matched with the resources to carry out people's expressed wishes then perhaps more people will be enabled to experience their own good death.

There are many legal and ethical difficulties to be resolved before living wills could become widely used, but the concept at least opens up the possibility of thinking and talking about death and dying and so could contribute to a breaking of the silence on the subject. The concept of the 'last will and testament' is changing too, and the legacy that people choose to leave their family and friends is often more than their financial assets. Dying people are seeking to leave behind remnants of themselves in a variety of ways – some in creative works, painting or poetry, others in letters or personal effects. In some hospices this need has been acknowledged – writers and artists in residence work with dying people both to enable them to express their feelings and fears about dying and also to leave an appropriate legacy for their loved ones.

There are indications that any taboos surrounding death and dying are breaking down and that the topic is one which we may all feel more comfortable with in the future. This is indeed to be welcomed if it enables us in both professional and private ways to be of help to dying and bereaved people.

References

Ariès, P. (1991) *Western Attitudes towards Death*, Marion Boyars, London.

Armstrong, D. (1987) 'Silence and Truth in Death and Dying', *Social Science and Medicine*, 24, 8.

Bowlby, J. (1969) *Attachment and Loss*, vol. 1: *Attachment* (1972); vol. 2, *Separation, Anxiety and Anger* (1980); vol. 3, *Loss, Sadness and Depression* (1982) Hogarth Press, London.

Buckman, R. (1988) *I Don't Know What to Say*, Macmillan, London.

Buckman, R. (1992) *How to Break Bad News: A Guide for Health-care Professionals*, Papermac, London.

Butler, R. N. (1963) 'The Life Review: An Interpretation of Reminiscence in the Aged', *Psychiatry*, 26, 65–76.

Cartwright, N. and Seale, C. (1990) *The Natural History of a Survey*, Institute for Social Studies in Medical Care, Kings Fund, London.

Elias, N. (1985) *The Loneliness of the Dying*, Basil Blackwell, Oxford.

Fallowfield, L. (1990), *The Quality of Life: The Missing Measurement in Health Care*, Souvenir Press, London.

Field, D. and James, N. (1993) 'Where and How People Die' in D. Clark, (ed.), *The Future for Palliative Care*, Open University Press, Buckingham.

Gorer, G. (1965) *Death, Grief and Mourning*, Creuset, London.

Green, J. and Green, M. (1992) *Dealing with Death: Practices and Procedures*, Chapman and Hall, London.

Henley, A. (1986) *Good Practice in Hospital Care for Dying Patients*, King Edward's Hospital Fund for London.

Hockey, J. (1990) *Experiences of Death: An Anthropological Account*, Edinburgh University Press, Edinburgh.

Jung, C. (1938) *Modern Man in Search of a Soul*, repr. RKP, London (1975)

Kohner, N. (1993) 'The Loss of a Baby: Parents' Needs and

Professional Practice after Early Loss', in D. Dickenson, and M. Johnson, (eds), *Death, Dying and Bereavement*, Sage, London.

Kubler-Ross, E. (1970) *On Death and Dying*, Tavistock, London.

Macguire, P. and Faulkner, A. (1988) 'Communicate with Cancer Patients: Handling Bad News and Difficult Questions', *BMJ*, 297, 2, 907–9.

Neale, B. (1993) 'Informal Care and Community Care', in D. Clark (ed.), *The Future for Palliative Care*, Open University Press, Buckingham.

Open University (1993) K260 *Death and Dying*, Open University, Milton Keynes.

Parkes, C. M. (1975) *Bereavement: Studies of Grief in Adult Life*, Pelican Books, London.

Parkes, C. M. (1988) 'Bereavement as a Psychosocial Transition: Processes of Adaptation to Change', *Journal of Social Issues*, 44, 3, 53–65.

Seale, C. (1993) 'Demographic Change and the Care of the Dying, 1969–1987' in D. Dickenson and M. Johnson (eds), *Death, Dying and Bereavement*, Sage, London.

Shapiro, J. (1989) *Ourselves, Growing Older: Women Ageing with Knowledge and Power*, Fontana/Collins, London.

Sheldon, F. (1993) 'The Needs to be Met' in *Needs Assessment for Hospice and Specialist Palliative Care Services: From Philosophy to Contracts*, National Council for Hospice and Specialist Palliative Care Services, Occasional Paper 4.

SMAC/SMNAC (1992) *The Principles and Provision of Palliative Care*, London.

Tookman, A. and Kurowska, A. (1993) *Palliative Care Handbook* (K260 Death and Dying), Open University, Milton Keynes.

Ward, B. and Houghton, J. (1987) *Good Grief: Exploring Feelings, Loss and Death with Over-11s and Adults*, CRUSE, London.

Williams, R. (1990) *Protestant Legacy: Attitudes to Death and Illness among Older Aberdonians*, Oxford University Press, Oxford.

Willson, J. W. (1989) *Funerals Without God: A Practical Guide to Non-religious Funerals*, The British Humanist Association, London.

Worden, J. W. (1983) *Grief Counselling and Grief Therapy*, Tavistock, London.

Wright, B. (1989) 'Sudden Death: Nurses' Reactions and Relatives' Opinions', *Bereavement Care*, 8, 1, Spring.

Yates, D. W., Ellison, G. and McGuiness, S. (1993) 'Care of the Suddenly Bereaved', in D. Dickenson and M. Johnson (eds), *Death, Dying and Bereavement*, Sage, London.

Index

Index